Excellence in Brand Communication

The ICA Guide to Best Practice

Brendon
Dow
Elder
Elwood
Fleischmann
Macaulay
Middleton
Mirlin
Rutherford
Stevenson
Young

Compiled and Edited by David Rutherford

Published by the **Institute of Communications & Advertising (ICA)**
2300 Yonge Street,
Suite 500-Box 2350
Toronto, Ontario
M4P 1E4
(416) 482-1396
www.ica-ad.com

ISBN 0-9697881-9-3

Printed and bound in Canada by University of Toronto Press.

First Edition

EXCELLENCE IN
BRAND COMMUNICATION

The ICA Guide to Best Practice

Compiled and Edited by David Rutherford

Based, in concept, on the UK publication *Excellence in Advertising*, edited by Leslie Butterfield.

Excellence in Brand Communication
The Origins

This book is Canadian, but it has a transatlantic family tree.

Its roots go back to the IPA's Seven Stages training program. The IPA is the Institute of Practitioners in Advertising in the UK, the equivalent of Canada's ICA. The IPA has a worldwide reputation for best practice. It was they, for example, who launched the IPA Effectiveness Awards in 1980—the first show in the world based on advertising's business effectiveness, as proven by a rigorous written case. This became the model for similar competitions in other countries, including the Cassies, which launched in Canada in 1993.[1] The Seven Stages program is another reflection of the IPA philosophy. It is an array of best practice courses, many given by "names" in the UK industry.

Leslie Butterfield is Chairman of one of the UK's top agencies, and was Chairman of the IPA's Training and Development Committee from 1989–1997. It was his idea to capture the Seven Stages program in a book. This led to *Excellence in Advertising*, which he compiled and edited. It has been extremely successful.

Our book owes a great debt to Leslie, and follows his idea of getting top names to share what they know. However, there are important differences. First, we needed to broaden the scope from advertising to "brand communication." Second, this is not the UK book with Canadian examples sprinkled here and there like raisins in cereal. It is entirely homegrown.

The objective, however, is the same. To help build stronger brands.

---

1 There are now over a 100 Canadian Advertising Success Stories. See www.cassies.ca.

The Chapters

Contributors

David Rutherford (Chapters One and Eight)

David graduated in the UK as a Civil Engineer, an affliction from which he has since recovered. He came to marketing via Procter & Gamble (Canada), where he worked on various major brands on the way to becoming the P&G equivalent of a Category Manager. Shortly thereafter, he left P&G and joined Ogilvy & Mather. At O&M he worked on a wide range of major brands, on the way to becoming President and Vice-Chairman in Toronto. In 1991, he became a consultant, specializing in marketing, advertising, and business writing. During that time, David has been heavily involved in the Cassies. As Editor, he has reviewed well over a hundred cases, and is the author of the Crossover Notes. These capture the lessons learned from all winning success stories, and can be found at www.cassies.ca. In other words, David has been in a brand-building environment for his entire career. He has seen the good, the bad, and the ugly, and passes on that experience in this book.

Peter Elwood (Chapter Two)

Peter retired, cheerfully and insouciantly, still comparatively young, after a stellar career with Unilever Canada. He had been President of Lipton and Lever Brothers, and VP of Marketing in both companies. He had a tour of duty in the UK, and has been active in a host of initiatives, including the Canadian Congress of Advertising, the Cassies, and Advertising Standards Canada. He started as an Assistant Brand

Manager at S.C. Johnson Wax, armed with an MBA from Western and a Chemical Engineering degree from Queen's. Peter is an inspirational leader with an impressive legacy, not only for successful brands, but also for grooming others to follow in his footsteps. In recognition of his achievements, he was awarded the ACA Gold Medal in 1995.

Andy Macaulay (Chapter Three)

Andy is one of three founding partners of the Toronto-based ideas company ZiG, whose clients include Corus Television, Danier Leather, Fidelity Investments, lavalife, Maple Leaf Foods, Sony, and Unilever. ZiG was named Agency of the Year in Canada in 2002 by Marketing Magazine. Prior to starting ZiG in 1999, Andy was Director of Strategic Planning and part-owner of Roche Macaulay & Partners of Toronto. From a standing start in 1991, that agency went on to win Marketing Magazine's Agency of the Decade for the 90s, Advertising Age's International Agency of the Year in 1998. It was also a four-time winner of Agency of the Year for Strategy Magazine in the 90s. Andy is a graduate of the Wilfrid Laurier University School of Business & Economics, and serves on the board of the ICA. He started his career in account management, but was always a planner at heart. As planning took hold in Canada he was one of the pioneers, and for this reason we asked him to give us his thoughts on advertising strategy.

Arthur Fleischmann (Chapter Four)

Arthur and four partners left Ammirati and Puris to open john st. in July 2001. The goal was to blend creative and strategic planning into a seamless process, leading to simple inspiring advertising that drives results. As President and CEO, Arthur turns his hand to everything, including moderating focus groups and throwing in a headline or two. The client roster includes Molson, Harvey's Restaurants, Scott Paper, Fujifilm, Astral Media, The Canadian Diabetes Association, and Lipton. The partners, who have worked together for nearly a decade, have been responsible for Cassies winners such as Clarica , Lipton Chicken Noodle Soup, Sunlight Detergent, and Lipton Sidekicks. Arthur spent seven years at Ammirati. He ran the Labatt's North American account, and launched the agency's strategic planning group, spearheading the planning model used by the team today. He then served as Managing

Director and President, COO. Prior to Ammirati, Arthur spent five years at Bates Canada, and several years at Kraft Foods New York. He holds a BA from Brandeis University and an MBA from the Kellogg Graduate School of Business at Northwestern University. Arthur also serves on the Board of Directors of the ICA.

Ian Mirlin (Chapter Five)

Ian was a copywriter and then Creative Director at several large multi-national agencies. He then became President and co-owner of his own agency for several years—Harrod & Mirlin (now FCB). The agency had an enviable reputation for delivering highly creative, highly effective advertising, and Ian has helped clients achieve meaningful results in almost every category imaginable. He has won many awards for creativity, but over and above this has been recognized by the industry with two Lifetime Achievement Awards: The Televison Bureau's Spiess Award and The Toronto Art Director's Club's Usherwood Award. Ian's wide-ranging background has given him a broad context for creativity in business today, and this is the theme of his chapter. Ian is currently Chief Creative Officer at Young & Rubicam (Canada).

Rupert Brendon (Chapter Six)

Rupert was in account management at Boase Massimi Pollitt/DDB and McCann Erickson in London before he came to Canada in 1967. He eventually became Chairman and CEO at DMB&B Canada—a position he held for sixteen years. The agency had been very small, but he took it to being a contender for the top ten by making "communications effectiveness" a single-minded goal. He was the author and editor of DMB&B's best-practice summaries (The Pocketpieces), which eventually ran to seventy-nine subjects. As a sign of their value, they were snapped up by his competitors and used for internal training. In 1983, Rupert founded NABS Canada. In 1993, he was the catalyst that brought the Cassies to Canada (based on the successful IPA Effectiveness Awards). More recently, he has spearheaded the Marketing Communications Education Trust (MCET) in an effort to raise the $5 million necessary to establish a Chair in Brand-Building at two Canadian universities. Rupert has been President & CEO of the Institute of Communications and Advertising since 1996. This book was his idea.

Lisa Elder (Chapter Seven)

Lisa joined Ogilvy & Mather Toronto as a newly minted Account Executive after graduating from Wilfrid Laurier University with an Honours degree in Business Administration. Over the next decade she rose to be Managing Partner: Head of Account Management and Consumer Insight. Throughout her career, Lisa had a keen instinct for the consumer, and she launched O&M's Consumer Inspiration Centre—making the consumer an integral part of creative development. Her passion for this fuelled her to open her own company, *heads up* **Inspiration from Information**®, in 1996. Since then, she has applied her talents to a wide range of clients, inventing unique ways to extract what is in the hearts and minds of consumers. She has also been active in sharing her learning. At the Canadian PMRS conference, June 2002, she was Best Speaker. At *Strategy Magazine's* Advertising Effectiveness Conference, December 2002, she conducted a senior client workshop on how to use qualitative research for greater advertising effectiveness. For the ICA, she has planned and moderated Canada-wide sessions on measuring advertising effectiveness—and she has been a key speaker at the ICA's premier Campaign Management training week at Queen's University.

Dr. Alan Middleton (Chapter Nine)

Alan has spent twenty-three years in marketing communications and twelve as a marketing academic and trainer. He has worked in marketing/advertising in the UK, the US, Norway, Japan, and Canada. His last two roles were as a Board Director of J. Walter Thompson (global) and President/CEO of its Japanese operation. Before that, he was President of Enterprise (now Enterprise Creative Selling) in Toronto. Alan did his MBA and Ph.D. at the Schulich School of Business, York University. He has taught at Schulich, the Rutgers Graduate School of Business in the US, the IDEA Graduate Business School in Buenos Aires, and the EMBA programs at Chiangmai University, NIDA, and Yonok College in Thailand. He is currently Executive Director of the Division of Executive Development, and Assistant Professor of Marketing at Schulich. He is involved with a plethora of organizations, for example as Chair of the *Marketing Magazine* Board of Advisors, co-founder of the Cassies, on the Marketing Committee of the United Way of Greater Toronto, on the Research Committee of the Ontario Tourism Marketing Partnership, and on the Branding Committee of the Toronto International Film Festival.

Laurie Young & Guy Stevenson (Chapter Ten)

Laurie is Managing Director of Ogilvy & Mather (Toronto). Perhaps as a precursor to her interest in Integrated Marketing Communication she established her career in media before moving into account management and then management. Much of Laurie's career has been at Ogilvy & Mather. O&M was one of the first to push beyond advertising alone—focusing on brand stewardship, with business-building campaigns that are discipline-neutral. Laurie has worked on virtually all of the agency's signature accounts, and champions business development. She, along with Guy Stevenson, has also been a pioneer in breaking down the silos that are such a stubborn feature of the business today. Laurie has an Honours B.A. degree from the University of Toronto, and a career-long commitment to professional standards, reflected in such activities as managing Ogilvy's training programs, and being a guest lecturer at the Rotman School of Business and the University of Alberta.

Guy is Managing Director of OgilvyOne Worldwide in Canada. He has eighteen years of direct marketing experience, including sixteen at OgilvyOne. In 2000, he was appointed to the worldwide board. Guy has worked on a wide range of accounts in business-to-business and consumer marketing, including such premier names as FedEx and American Express. Three years ago, he was responsible for a worldwide first in the Ogilvy global network—the launch of B2B Practice. This comprises senior executives available to provide high-level client consulting, and is indicative of Guy's keen interest in integrated marketing communication and brand-building.

Hugh Dow (Chapter Eleven)

Hugh came to Canada in 1967 from England. He joined MacLaren Advertising in 1969, becoming a Vice President in 1972, and Director of Media in 1974. In 1989 MacLaren was acquired by Lintas/Interpublic and Hugh launched Initiative Media—Canada's first media management company parented by an agency. Now M2 Universal, it is a free-standing business unit providing communication management services to MacLaren McCann clients and a growing list of others. M2 Universal is one of Canada's largest such companies with billings over $500 million. Hugh is the President. He is also immediate past chairman of The Print Measurement Bureau, and a Director and Past Chairman of ABC Audit Bureau of Circulations. He is four time President of the Canadian Media Directors' Council, a Director of BBM Bureau of Broadcast Measurement, and the current Chairman of the Medical Media Measurement Study. Hugh is widely quoted and his articles appear in many Canadian and U.S. trade publications. Strategy Magazine selected him as Media Director of the Year for three consecutive years in 2000, 2001 and 2002. He has also received the prestigious ACA Gold Medal for services to the advertising industry.

Foreword

It was as a teenager that I first met a bevy of art directors and writers—exotic and outspoken friends of my father. They said that advertising was the most fun you can have with your clothes on. I was hooked. The plan changed slightly when it became clear that I was not destined for the creative side of the business, but I got my foot in the door with an entry-level position in account management.

Advertising is not that complicated, I thought. I'll have the fundamentals in my pocket in a year or two. In fact, you never stop learning. For sixteen years I was CEO of Benton & Bowles in Canada (now part of Publicis), and I saw what it takes. You need exposure to an array of bosses, mentors, thought-leaders, clients, corporate philosophies, brands, and markets. Because advertising, like diplomacy, is the art of the possible.

Advertising has also changed. It is now total persuasive communication. We have to master a body of knowledge as daunting as in the legal or medical profession. But because our business is creative, it has fewer definitive answers. This is an ongoing challenge, but as Bernbach said, "Principles endure. Formulas don't." This book captures those principles.

Our authors are all leaders. They pass on a breadth of experience that is virtually impossible to accumulate these days. This will fast-track anyone in the business, and be a valuable addition to Brand Communication courses at universities.

My thanks to all contributors for their devotion to raising professional standards. And to the ICA for funding the book.

Rupert Brendon

About This Book

This book is for people earning their living in brand-building. It is based on experience rather than theory, but academics should enjoy the glimpse of how the other half lives. It is aimed at senior people, but the content is well worth reading at all levels.

Re-Evaluating Mental Models

Whether we realize it or not, we develop mental models to simplify complex situations. This is good up to a point, but the thinking can become entrenched. As you read, give your mental models an overhaul. Reinforce what's good, but rethink anything that has become hidebound.

Checklists

Brand-building is a lot more than painting by numbers. It takes analysis, insight, experience, talent, teamwork, stick-to-it-iveness, and often (though not always admitted) luck. There are quite a lot of checklists in this book, but we hope you'll read thoughtfully, extracting the lessons that go deeper than a litany of bullet points.

Chapter-Dipping

Chapters are self-contained, so by all means pick and choose. It's probably a good idea to read Chapter 1 first, because it sets up much of what follows.

Notes on Terminology

A product or service is not a brand. However, it creates clutter to keep making the distinction. Accordingly, we use *brand* as a catch-all, and *product* or *service* where the distinction needs to be stressed. In the same way, we use *advertising* in its usual sense, but also for "persuasive communication of all types." For "communication service providers," *partner* sometimes fits the bill. Elsewhere, we have pressed *agency* into service, giving it the broader meaning.

Practically every author refers to the explosion of terminology in the business. Rather than have conflicting definitions, we've used terms like *Brand Equity, Brand Essence, Brand Truth,* etc. in the commonly accepted way, with a meaning that should be clear from the context.

The same philosophy had guided *consumer* and *customer.* In packaged goods, consumers buy the product, and the trade are the customers. Other industries use *customer* to describe their clientele. Authors have used whatever reflects their background, but the meaning should be clear.

This book has already referred to the Cassies on page iv. These are Canadian Advertising Success Stories, demonstrated by a rigorous written case. You will also see reference to *Crossover Notes* in this book. These are an accumulating collection of lessons that "cross over" from one case to another—and since 2001 have been appended to each case at www.cassies.ca.

Finally, I hope you agree that we have kept jargon to a minimum, and told our story in clear, accessible, conversational English.

Acknowledgements

Whenever I read a page like this, I always have the wicked thought, "I bet they missed someone." Now it's my turn to run that gauntlet. We must start with what we owe Leslie Butterfield. When Rupert Brendon and I, jetlagged but otherwise in our right minds, shared our hopes with him, he gave us great encouragement, and steered us clear of potholes. Next our deep appreciation to the authors. They put their expertise on the line every day, but it's astonishingly time-consuming to write it out for a book—particularly when you have a passingly demanding day job.

The ICA staff were wonderful. Keeping multiple revisions on track—particularly through a file-destroying computer crash—bordered on heroism. Sandy Beglan also made me techno-savvy (up to a point, off a low base). Jani Yates improved the manuscript. And Jo-Ann McQuillan acted as project manager extraordinaire. Meanwhile, outside help came from Shelley Tigert, who acted as a copy editor during a short window of opportunity, and was extremely helpful in the time that she had. Rita Piazza then handled the indexing.

We thank Molson and Bensimon•Byrne for the cover, and the array of experts for their endorsements. If you're still reading this, it's customary now to see thanks to the long-suffering spouse and kids, but in our house they are perfectly happy to leave me cutting and pasting to my heart's content. Which, now that I think about it, is something we are all thankful for.

Finally, a word about the U of T Press. The birthing of a book like this can be quite turbulent. We thank them for their publishing midwifery.

Overview: Chapter One

If we were in any other line of work, we would not give brands a second thought. The general public never wonder why some brands are more appealing than others, much less torture themselves with questions about the essence of one brand or the key discriminator of another. Brands are part of everyday life, and that's it.

As we know, however, brands go much deeper, and this book's mission is to show how to turn this to business advantage. Some of the content will confirm what you believe. Some of it will challenge your thinking.

I also have to explain something that happened in writing this chapter. I kept running into an overlap between the concept of "a brand" and the idea of "positioning." It started to make everything too complicated, so I separated out an addendum called *Positioning and all that Jazz.*

Arthur Koestler was one of the first to study creativity in a formal way. He said that discovery is seeing something that was always there, but hidden from the eye by the blinkers of habit.

This first chapter re-interrogates what we might be taking for granted.

Chapter One

A Way to Think about Brand-Building

DAVID RUTHERFORD

Introduction

If you ask people when branding started, some will mention the arrival of Ivory Soap and Coca-Cola in the 19th century. Someone might suggest Lloyd's coffee house (the birthplace of Lloyd's insurance) in 17th century London. The branding of cattle will come up. But none of this goes back far enough.

The first case of branding occurred outside the Garden of Eden, and GOD was the brand manager. Cain had killed his brother Abel. It seems that the idea of an eye for an eye wasn't yet on the books, because GOD did not invoke the death penalty. Instead, he banished Cain, ordering him to wander the face of the earth. Cain did not go quietly. He complained to GOD that it was a wicked world out there. To protect him from that:

> The LORD set a mark upon Cain, lest
> any finding him should kill him. Genesis 4:15.

Branding is deeply imprinted into our brains. In prehistory, when we first got ourselves organized, we gave our leaders sceptres to symbolize power. Later, Roman legions fought under their own banners, and countries invented flags. Today, Supreme Court judges wear bizarre robes. And our kids dress up in cap and gown for graduation. All of this is a form of branding.

Coinage and banknotes reflect branding—with currencies having images as well as face value. The hallmark, around since the middle ages, is a brand in the purest sense—a mark that guarantees the value of the product.

There are books based on the idea that "you are a brand." I don't like the subtext—that packaging is more important than substance—but the impression you create certainly does open or close doors. Just look at news anchors and, at a more sobering level, studies that show that the image of the student affects the way teachers grade papers.

You may not have linked love at first sight to branding, but it is the most life-altering way that someone hits the sweet spot. Racism (a kind of hate-at-first-sight) is the sinister side of the same coin.

All of this is a clue as to why branding is so powerful.

Humans are not logical and dispassionate. We have an almost Pavlovian reflex to create values and meanings out of perceptions. There's probably an evolutionary explanation. The combination of intuition and logic served us well in a faceoff with a sabre-toothed tiger. So, the impulse to attribute values and meanings goes very deep. But, like everything else to do with the way our brains are wired, it is not a simple thing to manage.

Vulcans and Earthlings

There are no brands on Vulcan.

Vulcans are supremely intelligent and logical, and cannot be seduced by the siren call of branding. To a Vulcan, a product or service is the thing itself, at a price. Every decision is coolly reasoned. Reality is reality. Brands do not exist.

Earthlings are very different. I'll illustrate this from my days as a Brand Manager on Tide.

Tide was not the first detergent, but it overtook Unilever's Rinso to dominate the North American market. It was positioned for heavy-duty cleaning.[1]

---

[1] Whitening, colour care, all-temperature cleaning, and baby wash were picked off by Oxydol, Bold, Cheer, and Ivory Snow.

Tide was the big profit contributor, and Procter & Gamble (P&G) were obsessive about continuously improving it. Commentators said "all detergents are alike" but P&G knew this was not true, that over time users could pick up differences in performance. This led to multiple product improvements over the years. In effect, this was dealing with the Vulcan side of brand-building, and many improvements were not advertised. Meanwhile, we also spent a lot of time managing perceptions:

- Many consumers feel that sudsing equals cleaning. In fact, they are not that closely correlated, but a lot of work went into making the suds look right.
- The size of granules affects cleaning perceptions. This was closely managed.
- Brighteners make clothes *look* clean. They were expensive, but they were always a key part of the formula.
- Perfume used to smell pretty. Then we realized we were missing the opportunity to make clothes smell *clean.*
- Tide was a white powder. Should it have speckles? Research showed this could enhance a cleaning image. However, judgment prevailed—that Tide, as market leader, should not associate itself with such gimmicks.
- The packaging always looked powerful, and was updated with extreme care.
- Advertising stressed cleaning power and nothing else.[2]
- Customer questions and complaints were handled very seriously.

This shows that a brand is a mix of Reality and Perception—carefully managed, using knowledge, experience, research, and judgment.[3]

---

2 This was before emotional benefits were formally recognized. Intuitively, we also included a strong element of trust in Tide advertising.

3 They still stumble, of course, as Coca-Cola, Nike, Marlboro, Marks & Spencer, Apple, IBM, and others show. Overall, though, they manage Reality + Perception very well.

Earthling Hot Buttons

Strong brands hit our hot buttons. This is affected by some or all of the following:

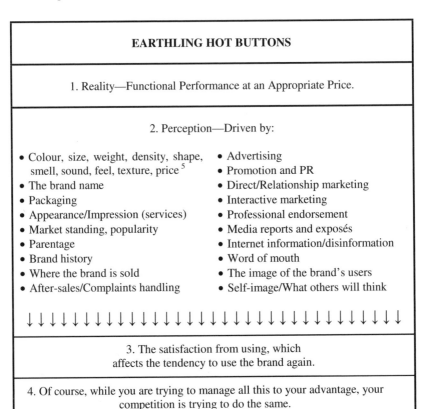

EARTHLING HOT BUTTONS

1. Reality—Functional Performance at an Appropriate Price.

2. Perception—Driven by:

- Colour, size, weight, density, shape, smell, sound, feel, texture, price [5]
- The brand name
- Packaging
- Appearance/Impression (services)
- Market standing, popularity
- Parentage
- Brand history
- Where the brand is sold
- After-sales/Complaints handling
- Advertising
- Promotion and PR
- Direct/Relationship marketing
- Interactive marketing
- Professional endorsement
- Media reports and exposés
- Internet information/disinformation
- Word of mouth
- The image of the brand's users
- Self-image/What others will think

↓↓↓↓↓↓↓↓↓↓↓↓↓↓↓↓↓↓↓↓↓↓↓↓↓↓↓↓↓↓↓↓↓↓↓↓↓

3. The satisfaction from using, which affects the tendency to use the brand again.

4. Of course, while you are trying to manage all this to your advantage, your competition is trying to do the same.

It's the sheer complexity of all this that makes marketing, advertising and all the other forms of persuasive communication so much fun but, on occasion, so hard to get right.

It would be fair to say that the rest of this book is devoted to that challenge.

---

5 Anything that appeals to the five senses for products, and the equivalent for services. Price can have a functional role and an image role.

The Idea of "Every Point of Contact"

We have an explosion of media options. This has led to the idea that you must manage, to your advantage, every interaction between your brand and its customers. The thinking isn't new (earlier marketers did it intuitively) but today it's more difficult.

There's a tendency to think of "every point of contact" in media terms, but EPOC goes way beyond this.[6] A phone call from a customer is a contact. So is the struggle to open a clumsily designed package. So is the impression left by a truck on the highway. So is using the product. Thinking in these terms can help when assessing the (sometimes chilling) cost of upgrading an underperforming product. It's easy to hope that customers are blissfully unaware, but an accumulation of small disappointments can be extremely dangerous.

If you are restaging a retail chain or hotel or airline, the idea of every point of contact can be helpful in other ways. You may assess that you have to create "the total brand experience" in one big splash, and if that's the case, you have to bite the bullet. But in some situations, you can to go in stages to spread out the cost.

When it comes to the media options, you have to decide where to invest—in established or new media, or both. It would make life easy if there were formulas for making these choices, but there aren't. The general approach is to dissect the task into its component parts, and then decide what is best suited to each part.[7]

A good feature of EPOC is that it does not presuppose where the answer lies. For example, advertising has been key to the success of many strong brands, but brands like Amazon.com and Microsoft have used advertising only sparingly. The key is to look at issues from the ground up, i.e. to be media-neutral.

---

6 There is a lengthy definition at the start of Chapter 9 by Alan Middleton.

7 In this sense "every point of contact" goes hand in hand with Integrated Communication. Chapters 9 and 10 discuss allocation of effort, but there are no pat answers.

Brand-Building—Simplified

Brand-building is not simple, but it's useful to have a mental picture of its most basic elements. I suggest something like this:[8]

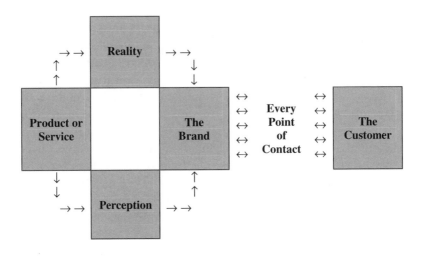

In words, it is along these lines:

Our tools are reality (performance + price) and perception. It's our job to find how to combine them in the most motivating way.

We must then manage every point of contact between the brand and its audiences, so that the most desirable customers choose our brand, and keep choosing it—and as a result we make the appropriate ROI.

---

8 The two-way arrows signify the brand *relationship*. An ingenious way to probe this is to ask the question, "What does the brand think of the customer?" [This idea came from a former colleague, Max Blackston, for many years with Research International.]

The Value of Brands

What we have been talking about only matters if brands are more valuable than the underlying product or service. They are.[9]

In packaged goods this is resoundingly highlighted by the blind and identified product test. A blind test will get a certain preference. The same test with the brands identified can get a very different result—for example a 45/55 blind-test loss can become a 60/40 identified preference. These differences have been found repeatedly, and they represent the values embodied in the brand.

It's harder to demonstrate the effect with services, but it's easy to imagine it. It's late at night, and you are driving around a strange and forbidding town, looking for a place to stay. Those name brand motels suddenly look a lot more inviting than the ones that belong in a Hitchcock movie.

The value to the brand owner shows itself in a number of ways, and the generally accepted benefits of a strong brand are:

a) Delivering current and future cash flow
b) Commanding a higher price
c) Delivering higher long-term profitability
d) Facilitating brand extensions
e) Improving customer loyalty
f) Buffering the brand from competitive attack
g) Getting or keeping the balance of power in your favour[10]
h) Motivating current staff
i) Attracting new talent
j) Potentially augmenting the stock price

---

9 This is not universally true, of course. A brand can be negative. The British Post Office is always near the top of the pack for awareness, and at the bottom for quality impression. My personal favourite (because of the transformation) is "made in Japan." At one time this meant shoddy, cheap, and copycat. How times have changed.

10 I don't see this discussed very often, but, not unlike a game of Monopoly, it's important to prevent a competitor from getting control of too much of the board.

It's clear that brands (strong brands, that is) have a financial value well above what a Vulcan might find logical. For example, about 60% of the market capitalization of Coca Cola can be attributed to brand value.

The most concrete expression of this occurs when brands change hands. When Nestlé took over Rowntree, they reflected a huge financial value for brands like Smarties, Aero, and Kit Kat. You may not have heard of Hamish Maxwell, but you do know the man who gave him his deep pockets—the Marlboro Cowboy. Maxwell was CEO of Philip Morris. After he snapped up Kraft and General Foods he gave a talk called *My $18 Billion Bet on Brands.* He explained why it was not a bet at all, because of the value of the Kraft and GF brands.

There is also the experience-based model. At P&G the value of brands was drummed in an article of faith. We were called Brand Managers, not Product Managers, and in that delightful P&G way we felt that made us a breed apart. It also explained why P&G, perhaps more than any other company, would not give up on a brand, even if it did poorly for years.

Companies like Interbrand publish tables of brand value, measured in financial terms.[11] David Haigh was Director of Brand Valuation at Interbrand before launching his own company in 1996. His publication *Brand Valuation: Measuring and Leveraging your Brand* is available from the ICA.

There is also the evidence that comes out of the PIMS (Profit Impact on Market Strategy) database. This is an unimpeachable source, started at General Electric in the mid-60s, expanded at the Management Science Institute at Harvard in the early 70s, and since 1975 developed by The Strategic Planning Institute. The findings are too detailed to cover here, but they show significant correlation between brand-building activity, share, profitability, and ROI.[12]

For most people, this establishes the *general* value of brands. A recent book edited by Leslie Butterfield—*AdValue: twenty ways that advertising works for business*—does this comprehensively.

---

11 The 60% figure for Coca-Cola came from one of their publications.
12 For PIMS-based papers, see Baxter, Biel, and Hillier in the Bibliography

The Idea of Brand Equity

Over and above accepting the general value of brands, business needs answers to more pointed questions—what brands to invest in, against what activity, and with good odds that it will all pay out. This is much more difficult to pin down.

There are various approaches. For primary decisions, companies can draw on ideas like the Boston Consulting Group matrix. For the marketing mix, they can use econometric models and other research techniques. But for many people the process is still heavily influenced by experience, rules of thumb, and judgment.

This brings up the idea of Brand Equity. Like many concepts, it has multiple meanings. There's the "end-audience" meaning, which roughly translates as "the sum total of all the (beneficial) things about the brand that the audience carries in their hearts and minds."

Then there is a hard-number financial meaning. This can be calculated, at least in broad terms. This led to the question, "What if we could measure financial Brand Equity, accurately, after every investment in product, promotion, advertising, etc.? The immediate figure, and the trend line, would tell us the cost-effectiveness of our investments."

When I was first at P&G I had a naïve notion along these lines. I wondered why a 60/40 preference in a blind-test couldn't be expressed in financial terms. I was quickly told that there are too many other variables. David A. Aaker is a brand expert from the academic/consulting world. He puts it like this:[13]

> The value of a brand cannot be measured precisely, but it can be estimated roughly (e.g. within +/– 30%). Because of this wide margin of error, such estimates cannot be used to evaluate marketing programs, but they can show that brand assets have been created.

---

13 *Brand Leadership*, page 16.

In other words, you can know that you have something valuable, but you can't know (in Brand Equity terms) if particular activities have worked or not.

If you think about it, this is why our line of work is a roller coaster. If Brand Equity could be measured precisely we would be like the captain on the bridge of a cruise ship, with computers malevolently humming away, and decision-making reduced to watching dials and pressing buttons.

We can, of course, go to the end-audience and measure Awareness, Salience, Differentiation, Esteem, Loyalty, Liking and so on.[14] When related to results in sales, share and profit we get a good idea of how different activities are doing, though there is still considerable room for interpretation. This is another source of thrills and spills.

When it comes to advertising, there are five main scenarios:

- The advertising is working, with visible value to the business.
- The advertising is working, but the effect is masked by other activity.
- The advertising is not yet working, but will, given time.
- The advertising is not working, but this is masked.
- The advertising is visibly not working.

All of these possibilities, except the first, cause angst, but the case for advertising is still strong. This is discussed in more detail in Chapter 8.

The Case to a Sceptical CFO

The body of evidence in favour of brand-building can never reach the level of a guarantee, but it is very much on the positive side of the ledger. If finance people push back, you can always ask them if they would guarantee the performance of a stock portfolio—but they may not appreciate the irony.

---

14 Many companies, agencies, and research houses have their preferred methods.

The Definition of a Brand

This isn't easy. In fact, I've never seen a definition that captures all the nuances. Here are various attempts, starting with one from Peter Doyle, who wrote the branding chapter for *Excellence in Advertising:*

> A name, symbol, design, or some combination, which identifies a product … as having a sustainable differential advantage.

John Philip Jones, in *What's in a Name*, goes beyond the product:

> A brand is a product that provides functional benefits plus added values that some consumers value enough to buy.

Charles Revson, of Revlon, stresses what happens in the mind:

> In the factory we make cosmetics, but in the store we sell hope.

Some capture the idea that a brand is a promise:

> A brand is a covenant….[15]

This one is out of the UK. (I wish I knew who said it):

> A brand is a bundle of meanings.[16]

I came up with one to stress the competitive angle:

> We manage reality + perception such that our brand comes out on top.

Finally, there are a host of definitions based on the idea of brand relationship.

---

15 Part of a longer definition by Jacques Chevron—see the next section.

16 This seems simple, but it is not. A brand, in order to get its hooks into our minds, has to be clearly positioned. But a brand also has texture. Just look at any image study. In other words, we have to tell the brand's story in a focused way, but we must also be mindful of the "bundle of meanings." There is more on this in the next section.

Building a Strong Brand

A brand is a lot more than a catchy slogan and an ad campaign. It is the result of "every point of contact" between the brand and its audiences. This leads to certain essentials for building a brand:

- *Relevant Differentiation.* No one sets out to create an irrelevant me-too, but in today's over-choiced world, it's easier said than done.
- *Knowledge and Esteem.* This is a combination of what customers know about the brand, their awareness, and how they feel.

  Note: these first two points borrow from Young & Rubicam's Brand Asset Valuator. This is a huge body of work, based on several hundred global brands, and several thousand local ones. According to published findings Relevance, Differentiation, Knowledge, and Esteem are all important, but Relevant Differentiation is the key. This suggests that awareness is not enough. New brands have to establish Relevant Differentiation first. And established brands, if they lose Relevant Differentiation, get into trouble, even if Knowledge and Esteem are high.

- *Quality and Service (at an appropriate price).* This is a blinding glimpse of the obvious, but it can be hard to deliver under pressure. The PIMS database shows that brands with high perceived quality deliver double the ROI of low quality brands.
- *Delivering what's promised.* Because we are Earthlings, a product that is superior on performance and price will not always do as well as a lesser one that's well marketed. Even so, it's dangerous to assume that clever marketing can compensate for a product or service that underdelivers.[17]
- *Accepting that a brand cannot be all things to all people.* Everyone agrees, but it's easy to waver at decision time. The political analogy is useful. Parties know that some people will never vote for them, some always will, and others will be amenable if the message is right. Brands are similar. We should not lose sleep if we do not appeal to people who will not buy us anyway.

---

17 We should never forget the way a host of North America brands were pole-axed by better-quality Japanese and European imports

- *Appealing to a big enough audience.* Sometimes, in the hunt for relevant differentiation, we can niche a brand into a corner.
- *Staying the course, and staying fresh.* Brands need continued support.[18] In addition, because they are part of a relationship, they must be trustworthy, consistent, and fresh. It is something of an oxymoron to be consistent and fresh at the same time, and this can lead to big disagreements. There is more on this in *Positioning and all that Jazz.*
- *Making sure the brand is understood, internally.* Explain the brand in a way that everyone will embrace. In an "every point of contact" world, don't leave this to chance.[19]
- *Having a powerful brand guardian.* Some clients have this as a high-level position, such as Chief Branding Officer. Most agencies have some version of it. The point is that if responsibility is spread across many people, it's difficult (some say impossible) to keep a brand on track.

Deciding What the Brand Stands For

A brand is valuable because, for a combination of factors, customers choose it, and keep choosing it, in preference to their other options.[20]

Deciding on that combination of factors (real and perceived) opens up an expedition through the wilds of Positioning, Focus of Sale, USP, Basic Stance, Key Consumer Benefit etc., to say nothing of Brand Equity, Brand Essence, Brand Truth, Brand Soul, Brand Identity, Brand Personality, Brand Character, Brand Image, and so on. These concepts mean different things to different people.[21] Also, we are often (sometimes unwittingly) working to different brand-building models.

---

18 Once you have built up brand strength, the brand does not disappear off the face of the earth if you cut back support for a while. The problems show up a year or two down the road, by which time the decision-makers have often moved on.

19 This goes way beyond meetings, memos, and e-flashes. See the extraordinary example from British Airways in Chapter 10.

20 It says "other options" to make sure we think through all the choices. In some categories the most likely option is to do nothing, and the competitor is inertia. This is the Frame of Reference decision. For example, with Campbell's Soup, does it compete in liquid soup, all soup, home-cooked food, or perhaps an emotional territory like comfort food?

21 I used to get fussed over Brand Character versus Brand Personality (Character = deep; Personality = shallow) but now see them as interchangeable.

We referred earlier to David Aaker. His books—*Managing Brand Equity, Building Strong Brands,* and *Brand Leadership*—are packed with case histories, charts, and diagrams. He covers multi-brands, master-brands, sub-brands, line-extensions, etc., essentially from the business manager's point of view.

There's Scott Bedbury in *A New Brand World* and Jon Steel in *Truth, Lies & Advertising.* They are more intuitive, perhaps reflecting their agency background. They have no charts and diagrams, and see brands as part of life. They probe for deep "brand truths" from the relationship point of view.

Then there is Jacques Chevron, a US-based consultant originally from Europe. He agrees that marketing hinges on meeting customer needs, but says brand-building has more to do with what the *company* believes. He sums this up with the quote:

Marketing begins with the customer. Branding begins at home.

He also tidies up the paradox: If great brands are a "bundle of meanings," why is a single-minded positioning seen to be so important?

He makes a distinction between marketing and brand-building. In his model, marketing must have a focused positioning, because that's what it takes to cut through the clutter. But branding is different. It is a consuming commitment to live the Brand Character. This is not a handful of catchy adjectives, but the values the company holds dear (about itself, its brand, and its customers). He says a brand has to be anchored to these deep-rooted beliefs to be successful.[22]

Finally, all the agencies, and many clients, have their own models. Some are quite elaborate, but they all hark back to a marvelous quote from the man who gave us "At Speedy You're a Somebody."

Find the greed, and fill the need—Jerry Goodis

---

22 These few paragraphs do not do justice to Chevron's thinking. You will get a better idea by reading *Marketing versus Branding* and other articles at http://jrcanda.com.

Whatever your process, though, the following are worth factoring in:

- *Clarifying the objective.* Usually, you are looking for the combination of Reality + Perception that will convince your target to choose, and keep choosing, your brand over their other options.
- *Looking for a gap.* It may be self-evident (Crest with fluoride to fight cavities) or hard to see (who knew that humanity needed a Walkman?). It may involve catching a trend, as when Listerine shifted from fresh breath to healthy gums. It may be in emotional territory that no one has tapped before.
- *Meeting an unmet need, or getting into a dogfight.* If there's attractive undefended territory, seize it. But the best real estate is often taken. Some people say you should not go head-to-head in this situation. This is not correct. It may still be your best option—you just have to find a way to win.[23]
- *Changing the goalposts.* Kudos to the unnamed genius who decided to change the name of Death Insurance to Life Insurance.
- *Taking into account what your audience already believes.* It's hard, but not impossible, to shift entrenched beliefs. (Marlboro was once a women's cigarette.) But Wisk was handcuffed for years by Ring around the Collar, despite many repositionings against whole-wash cleaning. In these situations, budget, time, and the client's appetite for risk all play a role.
- *Bringing brand equity, brand essence (and related ideas) to the table.* These are more complex ideas than the old "positioning" thinking, but they help get at the deeper forces driving a brand.
- *Deciding how relevant differentiation can be sustained.* This is rarely locked up in a patent. It usually has to be created and perpetuated by the sum of the brand's marketing activity. Advertising often plays a major role here.

---

23 See "More About the Head-On Attack" in *Positioning and all that Jazz.*

- *Resolving Unique Selling Proposition versus Unique Emotional Proposition.*[24] USP has been around for fifty years. But as products become similar, it's harder to find USPs, and you can finish up latching onto marginal features. Those in the UEP camp see the emotional connection as the key. To them, the USP is a needle in a haystack, and a blunt one at that.

- *Resolving Single-Mindedness versus Bundle of Meanings.* There are various ways to deal with the paradox:

  a) One is to define the bundle as a single entity. Volvo = Safety.
  b) Another is the "Focus of Sale" approach. The brand is defined in all its texture, but any given piece of communication has to be focused.
  c) There is Jacques Chevron's approach, which is a variant of (b). He uses Ben & Jerry's as an example. The ice cream has exotic ingredients—the focus of sale. But the *brand* is much more than this. It is rooted in the character and values of Ben and Jerry themselves, and the aura caused by their New England location.[25]
  d) Sometimes the bundle is a product benefit with an emotional added value. The totality is still single-minded, however. Tylenol illustrates this with "Take comfort in our strength."[26]
  e) Sometimes (I stared long and hard at the screen before writing this) the answer is a bundle.[27]

- *Remembering Freud.* In all of this, we should not forget that sometimes a cigar is just a cigar. Not every brand is anchored to a deep resonant truth, though it's surprising how many are.

---

24 I don't know if he coined UEP, but John Bartle uses it in *Excellence in Advertising.*
25 This ties back to "every point of contact." Advertising can focus on the ice cream, while the broader story can come from other sources.
26 I'm using the slogan as shorthand. In general, I'm from the school that says "what the brand stands for" should be in clear everyday English, not ad language.
27 I hesitated, because if this is taken wrongly it will do more harm than good. Usually, as it says in Chapter 8, we have to "feel the pain of leaving things out." But once in a while a brand can't be reduced to a single thought. "Tastes Great. Less Filling." is an example.

Capturing What the Brand Means

It can be tough to get the essence of a brand down to a few words. Some people think that you *must*, and the archetypes are brilliant:

• Apple = Radical Ease of Use
• Nike = Authentic Athletic Performance

Others feel that "the brand" cannot be captured so neatly, and favour something more descriptive, perhaps including visuals, music etc. to complete the picture. Whatever method you use, though, the brand must be clearly defined as to what it is, and what it is not. [For more on this, see Chapters 3 and 4.]

A Comment on Life-Cycle Theory

Many business schools, and some clients, believe in life-cycles. The favourite victim is the buggy whip. There must be some situations where brand-death is unavoidable, but it is a destructive, self-fulfilling prophecy.

The issue turns on the difference between product and brand. The product can change repeatedly over the years (though in cases like Classic Coke even this can be a mistake). The brand, however, is an enduring entity to be evolved. Let's look again at the buggy whip.

Suppose the leading brand was called Excalibur. It was made of leather. It was something you held in your hand. When cars came along, the company could easily have produced a top-of-the-line Excalibur driving glove. What about the goggles and sunglasses people wore in those open cars? They could have been Excalibur. So could the blankets that people wrapped themselves in.

Excalibur could easily have been the brand for the new, well-heeled automotive class. This is why brands are so valuable, and life-cycle theory is so pernicious.[28]

---

28 If you think this is a stretch, recall that P&G started off making soap and candles. They phased out candles in the 20s, but somehow managed to survive.

The Role of Advertising in Brand-Building

Let's start with a definition based on what we've covered:

> In brand-building, we want to imprint a mix of Reality + Perceptions in the minds of desirable customers, such that they choose our brand, and continue to choose it, over their other options.

This mix gets into the mind in different ways. Some recent brands (Amazon.com and Microsoft have been mentioned) hardly needed advertising at all. Marks & Spencer in the UK is a longer-standing example. They started in the 1800s as a stall in a street market. Now they are a UK institution.

M&S sold middle-of-the-road clothing, and later excellent food, with an obsession for quality at a fair price, and very little brand advertising. Success was built more on Reality than Perceptions, and this created generations of satisfied customers.[29]

That said, advertising often has a major role in brand success.[30] This is for four main reasons:

a) It communicates Reality.
b) It builds Perceptions.
c) It delivers Unique Emotional Propositions.
d) As a result, it is excellent at establishing the foundation of strong brands: Relevance, Differentiation, Knowledge, Esteem.

This assumes, of course, that the advertising is done well—on strategy, effective, and appropriately supported. John Bartle is one of the principals at the UK agency Bartle Bogle Hegarty. They have a superb track record for brand-building advertising, with many IPA Effectiveness Awards. He sums it up like this:

> Advertising has a unique role in building brands, because it appeals to the head and the heart.

---

29 Don't be distracted by the fact that M&S recently went through the doldrums. As mentioned earlier, even powerful brands get into trouble. In the M&S case they did not see that their middle-of-the-road clothing had become frumpy.

30 The Cassies, the IPA Effectiveness Awards, and the Effies provide ample evidence.

What Does It All Mean?

I was at P&G when I first started to grasp what brands are all about, and I found it thrilling. But I had this nagging question, "What do I actually do?" It took me a while to turn this into a practical list, but you might find the following useful:

1. See the brand as more important than anything else.
2. Think like a parent, raising a bright but unruly child.
3. Think like a Vulcan *and* an Earthling.
4. Manage Reality *and* Perception at every point of contact.
5. Do not make change for change's sake.
6. But still challenge the tried and true.
7. If the brand stumbles, solve the right problem, not the easy one.
8. If the brand is doing well, find ways to do even better.
9. Find brilliant solutions—inspire them, create them, approve them, but above all, get them into the marketplace.
10. Hand over a brand that is stronger than the one you inherited.

We have different roles. We hope this book will help in all of them.

Positioning and All That Jazz

An Addendum to *A Way to Think About Brand-Building*

DAVID RUTHERFORD

Introduction

Nowadays most companies and agencies work to some sort of "brand" model.

The key point about brands is that although they are products like Maxwell House and services like Federal Express, they aren't concrete at all. They are a set of beliefs and feelings in the mind. At one level, we all understand this. In 1879, without help from branding or name-generation experts, Harley Procter of P&G had a brainwave in church, and decided to call his white soap "Ivory." The name had a host of positive connotations. It was a stroke of branding genius.

Great brands capture a place in the consumer's mind (and heart) better than the also-rans. The main way to do this used to be through some combination of:

- The Product or Service itself
- Name
- Package, or the equivalent for services
- Availability
- Advertising
- Reputation of the brand owner

These days we see things in a more complex way, and so you may have felt a slight shudder of disagreement in reading this list. But that's the way it used to be, as many of today's household names rose to the top.

The Idea of Positioning

Around the 60s the idea of positioning started to take hold. You've no doubt heard of (if not read) Trout & Ries. The notion of staking out a territory in the consumer's mind was not new (it had been well entrenched at P&G for years), but Trout & Ries codified the idea and marketed it—in effect positioning *positioning* to a receptive business community.

The basics have become familiar—that the battle is for the best real estate in the consumer's mind, and that if we don't take into account how the mind works, and how overloaded it is, we will fail.

Part of the Trout & Ries mission was to make positioning blindingly simple. Once in a while (in my view) they overdo this, but they are right about the following:

a) To win the battle for the mind a brand has to be sharply defined.[1]
b) What people already believe has a big effect on what you can get them to believe.
c) It is a huge advantage if you can stake out your territory first.

They drove home the importance of being sharply defined by suggesting that brands could be captured in one word. A typical list looked like this, and the "one word" idea is still around today:

- Tide = Clean
- Crest = Cavity Prevention
- Volvo = Safety
- Coke = Refreshment
- Pepsi = Youth
- Marlboro = Masculinity[2]

In terms of point (b), we know that the consumer's mind is not a blank slate. Looked at another way, the fact that it's hard to shift existing impressions is one of the reasons that established brands are so hard to knock off their perch.

---

1 I prefer "sharply defined" to "single-minded" for reasons that we will come to.
2 This list shows that "one word," though good for focus, is simplistic. Coke, Pepsi, and Marlboro (in fact most brands) are too complex to be captured by one word.

Point (c) is valid, though Trout & Ries have had to be careful in defining what they mean by "first." Many people believe that you have to be first to market (and all things being equal that is a great advantage.) However, any number of market leaders did not do this. Pampers, McDonald's, Kleenex, IBM, and Downy all found others had set up camp first. Trout & Ries resolve this by saying that the brand has to be "first into the mind."[3]

The Many Meanings of Positioning

In ordinary English *positioning* means putting something, by choice, in a particular place (as in positioning a clock in the centre of mantelpiece). In much the same way we say that one of the roles of advertising is "to help position a product in the consumer's mind." This is a general meaning.

There is also what I call the "chessboard" meaning. You look at a market, and conclude, "We need to position a brand in the low-calorie segment."

This chessboard meaning can lead to an odd play on words. For example, the comment above led to the question, "Yes, but how should we *position* it?"

This question is going deeper than just identifying a square on the board. It is getting at what the brand should stand for.

In some of the big marketing companies, especially in packaged goods, this took shape as the "Positioning Sentence." The idea was to force decisions about the target, the competitive frame, the promise or benefit, and the point of difference. At its core, it is a "benefit/reason-why" statement, and it goes like this:

> To such and such a defined audience, Excalibur is the brand of (competitive frame) that promises (the single-most compelling benefit) with the (single-most compelling point of difference).

---

3 This is important when deciding whether to attack a competitor, or look for another positioning option. As noted in the main part of this chapter, there are some who are queasy about the head-on attack. I think it can be the right and necessary thing to do. We come to this later.

An old General Foods document captured it like this:

> To caffeine-concerned coffee drinkers, Sanka is the brand of coffee that promises unsurpassed[4] relief from the effects of caffeine because it has no caffeine to upset you.

Reading this today, it seems circuitous. But Sanka was at one time the dominant brand of decaf, so much so that (like Xerox, Thermos, and Hoover) it became the everyday generic word for the category.

The Positioning Sentence requires some important decisions. The frame of reference is "brand of coffee" i.e. Sanka is competing against all coffees—not just decaffeinated coffees. The benefit is "unsurpassed relief…" Conspicuously, there is no mention of taste or enjoyment or any of the emotional benefits of coffee.[5]

The Positioning Sentence then evolved into the Positioning Statement. It was the same thinking, without the cumbersome language. It went something like this:

> Sanka promises caffeine-concerned coffee drinkers unsurpassed relief from the effects of caffeine, because it is caffeine free.

From Simplicity to Complexity

Sometime in the 70s Brand Personality (and Brand Character) arrived. At that time, Positioning Statements were still simple, with the focus on a functional benefit. Brand Personality introduced a harder-to-define aspect of what a brand stands for. This caused angst. Some Positioning Statements expanded to include it. Others left it to float in the firmament between Creative Strategy and Execution. Positioning started to get complicated.

Emotional benefits were not far behind. I was at P&G when one of

---

4 This is "aggressive parity." It's invaluable when you can't claim superiority in a Vulcan sense, but want to leave that impression with Earthlings.

5 This is single-mindedness riding rough-shod over common sense. I can hear the poor soul, wanting to include taste in the Positioning, being shot down because "that wouldn't be single-minded." But single-mindedness can lead you astray. Consumers want "Great coffee without the caffeine." Is that so complicated? This is why I prefer "sharply defined" to "single-minded." Focus is always crucial, but "one word" is not always right.

the agencies proposed that "meaning and value extensions" played a big role.[6] The Emotional Benefit started to find its way into mainstream thinking, but there was a problem. Positioning clung to its functional roots—so there was no neat and tidy way to add the emotional benefit in. They also brought a "single-mindedness" problem. There was a best-practice document (I saw it at three of the packaged goods companies) that said a brand should (1) have a key functional benefit, (2) have a key emotional benefit, (3) have a reason why for both, and (4) still be single-minded!

Perhaps not surprisingly, being single-minded was more than some could bear. Positioning Statements started to become a laundry list of Features and Benefits and Reasons Why. In some cases they even ventured into the esoteric uplands of Values. Creative people threw up their hands. One of my colleagues (Richard Fowler) came up with a brilliant question to deal with such a laundry list:

> Please, can you tell me what do you want me to have an idea about?

This was partly answered by the arrival of Focus of Sale. The thinking went roughly like this (I'm being tongue-in-cheek, of course):

> A Positioning Statement should be so sharply defined that it is obvious where to focus—but just in case it isn't, here's something to clarify the situation: the Focus of Sale.

Then another complication arrived. Manufacturers started to feel that it was too expensive and risky to launch self-standing brands.[7] This led to a host of line-extensions, and the need to subdivide brands into umbrella brands, master brands, sub-brands and so on. Positioning now had to accommodate not just a single brand, but the whole family tree.

So an idea that started as the essence of simplicity had become a conundrum. People struggled to make all the pieces fit together, and to some extent still do.

---

6 They meant "With Pampers, you feel like a good mother."

7 Some companies like Kraft and Heinz used a corporate name as an umbrella, but the majority view at this time was in favour of self-standing brands.

Volvo, Sanka, and Crest

Some of the difficulties with Positioning (as it has been practiced) come to light when we look at these major brands. At one point Volvo was the poster-child for the one-word approach. Volvos are safe. They look safe. Product improvement was always about safety. So was their advertising. Even the Volvo customer, with their sensible lifestyle, seemed "safe." This was successful for many years.

But stodginess came along for the ride.

Volvo has since decided that they can no longer be a box on wheels. This raises the question: could the stodginess problem have been headed off at the pass? Conventional positioning thinking would have a lot of trouble with this, because "safe and sporty" is an oxymoron. But Volvo are going for it.[8] The first step, of course, has been in the product, and it will be a long haul. But I have been told that the new, more exciting positioning is taking hold.

The Sanka story is similar. They were so caffeine-focused that they created a medicinal image for themselves.

Crest illustrates a different point. It was the first brand to stake out cavity prevention (with the seal of approval from the American and Canadian Dental Associations). As a result, it dominated North American toothpaste for a generation. Eventually, though, all toothpastes got fluoride, as did the water supply. Cavities started to disappear. Crest's reason-for-being was slipping away.

From a positioning point of view, it was clear that Crest would have to find the new high ground. This was emerging as "mouth health," an elusive concept related to plaque and tartar control, and healthy gums. In an ideal world (from the Crest point of view) they would develop the right product for mouth health, and shift to the new positioning. But Colgate, who had always played catch-up in cavity prevention, beat them to the punch with Colgate Total. With this product, good marketing, and Dental Association endorsement, Colgate took over as #1, and Crest found themselves playing catch-up with Crest Complete.[9]

---

8 They coined the word "Revolvolution" to help get the new idea across.

9 The story isn't over. All the top brands are now frantically pushing whiteness. Ironically, Crest took the market *away* from whitening when it knocked Pepsodent off its perch years ago. Pepsodent had clambered to #1 with the notorious jingle, "You'll wonder where the yellow went when you brush your teeth with Pepsodent."

There is a thread running through these stories. If brands don't carve out a strong position and stick with it they lose out because the customer does not know what they stand for. But if they do not adjust in the face of change, they also lose out. In principle, Positioning is supposed to be sufficiently supple to deal with this. In practice, the thinking can be overly rigid.

The Rearrival of "The Brand"

Sometime during the late 80s the idea of "the brand" started to take hold again. It had been around for a 100 years or more. But marketers and advertisers had (unwittingly) been taking brands for granted.

Some years before, Peter Drucker shook decision-makers out of their pre-set notions by asking the devastatingly simple question, "What business are you in?"

This time, some leading thinkers, many on the advertising side, asked, "Do we understand the brand?" The response was, "Yes, of course," but under scrutiny it turned out that there was a lot more to brands than we had realized.[10]

As the brand way of thinking re-emerged, it was not all smooth sailing. Partly because of the recession in the early 90s, and partly because of private labels, some famous brands got into trouble.[11] For a time there was the notion that brands had outlived their usefulness. But they weathered the storm, and since then the brand approach is almost universally seen as the key to long-term success.

Relating "The Brand" to Positioning

In fact, these are two sides of the same coin:

- Both are based on winning the battle for the consumer's mind.
- Both are based on sustained competitive advantage.
- Both have to take into account what the customer can—by marketing activity—be persuaded to believe.

---

10 This thinking was very much part of the Planning revolution that started in the UK.

11 The defining moment was April 2, 1993 when Marlboro in the US cut its price by 40 cents a pack, and lost $13.4 billion in stock market value.

- Both are based on the idea that "what the brand stands for" must be reflected at every point of contact.
- Both are long term—i.e. they reflect the belief that if a brand flits around, customers will not establish the relationship and trust needed for success.

From this, it's hard to see how they differ at all. But there are two big distinctions:

a) Positioning is not overly concerned with the rich texture that makes up a brand. It tries to be single-minded, or if not this, sharply focused.

b) The brand approach spends a lot of time trying to understand the relationship between brand and customer, to find brand truths, and so on. In this sense, it is not as precisely defined. Hence the quote, "a brand is a bundle of meanings."

Overlap with Creative Strategy

On hearing one of Mozart's operas, the Austrian Emperor Joseph II said, "Too many notes, my dear Mozart." He was wrong about the opera, but in our line of work there *are* too many concepts chasing down similar ideas.

The overlap can be confusing. We've seen that Positioning and Branding have a great deal in common. What about Creative Strategy? This is very close too, as Andy Macaulay explains in Chapter 3.

A Particular Meaning of "Creative Strategy"

There aren't many jokes about language and vocabulary, but here's my favourite:

Q: What's the difference between ignorance and apathy?
A: I don't know. And I don't care.

This isn't true with "Creative Strategy." Some people care intensely about how the term is used, particularly because of an anomalous usage that came out of the packaged goods companies. I'll try to clarify that here.

In plain English, *Objective, Strategy* and *Tactics* relate to each other as follows:

a) *Objective.* The goal, as in, "I will win this chess match so decisively that it shakes my opponent's confidence for the rest of the tournament."
b) *Strategy.* The idea guiding the plan, as in, "I will keep the position very complicated, and put him under heavy time pressure."[12]
c) *Tactics.* What you do to execute the plan (therefore sometimes called execution) as in, "I will open with the Nimrod Attack."

The typical marketing plan uses these same meanings:

a) Marketing Objective[13]
b) Marketing Strategy (the path to achieve the objective)
c) Tactics (the activities that execute the strategy)

So far so good.

But when you build a Marketing Plan, you have to set objectives for each part of the marketing mix. The packaged goods companies called these objectives "strategy" because they are a subset of the Marketing Strategy. It went like this:

Product Strategy	Packaging Strategy	Pricing Strategy	Creative Strategy	Media Plan[14]	Promotion Strategy	Trade Strategy	Spending Strategy

---

12 In competitive situations, you are usually looking for a way to apply your strength against the opponent's weakness. See Chapter 3.
13 Generally a statement about shipments, share and profit. Sometimes also a more qualitative goal, such as "be seen as the undisputed leader."
14 By custom, "The Media Plan" contained the Media Objectives and the Media Strategy.

In ordinary English, *strategy* is a "how" word, but in this approach "Creative Strategy" means "what we intend to say" and not "how we intend to say it." The short-hand for this has therefore become:

Creative Strategy   = WHAT we say
Creative Execution = HOW we say it

For example, Crest had a famous long-running campaign against the cavity positioning. For them, the WHAT and HOW were:

Creative Strategy   = Cavity prevention
Creative Execution = "Look Ma, no cavities."

Note that the Positioning and Creative Strategy use the same words—cavity prevention. Some people find this confusing, but it's only a version of "too many notes." The problem never occurred at P&G because we used the Creative Strategy to define what the brand stood for.

This special usage of "Creative Strategy" is alive today. The documents in many systems are called "Creative Strategy" even though they are preoccupied with the WHAT more than the HOW. Some people, of course, use "strategy" with its everyday meaning, and say, "We want to convince people that Superbo is the best thing since sliced bread, and our strategy is to use Italian chefs as spokespeople." This is the "how" meaning, and is not wrong, but it is like nails on a blackboard to people who restrict "Creative Strategy" to its special meaning.

More on "Too Many Notes"

I recently came across the "brand" thinking of a big company. It was a rather attractive circular diagram made up of:

- Brand Essence
- Functional Ability
- Points of Difference
- Source of Authority (a clever version of Reason Why)
- Personality
- Predominance (the edge over competition)
- Mandatory Branding Elements
- Product Position (this must be their word for Positioning)
- Brand Character

Another company's system has most of the above, plus:

- Values
- Insight
- Functional and/or Emotional Benefit.

All of these concepts are important, but I'm reminded of something David Ogilvy once said about all this. He wondered, with a heavy dose of irony, how he and his colleagues ever managed to come up with successful campaigns—being, as they were, denied such enlightenment.

If you find it hard to carry all these concepts in your head, the following might be useful. Successful brands embody three things that all happen to begin with D, allowing what I call the 3-D point of view:

The benefit is	**D**	esirable
The brand		elivers
The brand is		istinctive[15]

© David Rutherford Strategy Consulting

The need for a *desirable benefit* is self-evident. It may be functional, or emotional, or both.

Secondly the brand must *deliver.* P.T. Barnum built a business believing there's a sucker born every minute, but that's not a good idea today.

Finally, there's *distinctiveness.* Some people (wrongly) think the *benefit* has to be distinctive. This is often a miscall, as we shall see.

---

15 Note that it says *the brand* is distinctive, not the benefit. The reason is coming.

Where Does Distinctiveness Come From?

A brand must have "Sustainable Relevant Differentiation," but on what basis?

- Some brands are better mousetraps from a Vulcan point of view, with the distinctiveness in the product or service itself. This will usually become the focus of marketing effort, though not always.[16]
- Market leaders usually own the category benefit. By definition, this benefit is not distinctive. Distinctiveness comes from *how* they stake out the territory.
- Distinctiveness can come from being first into the mind. This includes the pre-emptive benefit—something that anybody *could* say, but you say first. MasterCard. Don't leave home without it.
- Products can be similar, with distinctiveness coming from the reason-why, or the more elegant version of this, "permission to believe." Victor Kiam liked Remington razors so much he bought the company.
- It can come from the emotional benefit. For Pampers this has been, "You are a good mother." For Huggies, "Your baby is happy." These are very different ways of hitting the sweet spot.
- It can come from packaging (L'Eggs) and other marketing effort.
- It can come from advertising.
- It can, and often does, come from what has been called "brand equity in the head." This is the elusive combination of the above, plus name, reputation, personality, brand properties, and other branding elements.

The idea that the benefit has to be distinctive comes from USP thinking. It's obviously not wrong to pin everything on a unique benefit, if it's the right one. But this can lead you to the wrong answer. Far better is to make the *brand* distinctive, by whatever means will work best.

---

16 I was once Brand Manager on Downy. For years, we never mentioned softening in advertising, building the business with a long-running campaign on April Fresh Smell.

More About the Head-on Attack

The idea behind Positioning, or "the Brand," or the 3-D concept, is to get control of the most valuable square on the board. It is a huge advantage to be "first into the mind," so what do you do if a competitor gets there first?

Some believe that you should not attack an entrenched competitor.[17] Of course, it doesn't make sense to take on the bully in the schoolyard if you are going to get thrashed, but I would still like to refute this view with a number of examples.

At one time I worked on Duracell. It was the first alkaline battery. It snatched the high ground of "long lasting." It was distinctive because it was the Coppertop. It was a better mousetrap compared to existing batteries—*No other battery looks like it, or lasts like it*—and it quickly went to #1.

Then Energizer came along. From a Vulcan point of view, it was pretty much equal to Duracell. For many years, though, it did not fight Duracell on long-lasting. This was seen as a me-too strategy. Duracell flourished, and Energizer malingered. Eventually, someone (in the US, I think) threw out the me-too worry, and decided to attack. The Energizer Bunny has been going and going ever since. There are three important points here:

a) It's wrong to attack with a weak proposition, but that does not mean it is wrong to attack at all.
b) When you attack, the battle is not about Creative Strategy (the WHAT). It is about Execution (the HOW).
c) Distinctiveness is not in the benefit, but in the execution. Duracell told its story with toys, with the bing-bang-bong Coppertop mnemonic. Energizer had the Bunny.

Duracell withstood the Bunny for some time (a testament to being "first into the mind") but I've been told that over the long haul Energizer has made significant inroads into Duracell's #1 position.

---

17 I've heard this from clients, colleagues, and marketing professors.

Now to Dove. In 1991, Dove and Ivory had equal #1 dollar shares in the bar soap market. Dove had built its business on a superior formula (it was not a soap, and had said for years, "Dove won't dry your face the way soap can.") Ivory, for as long as anyone could remember, had stood for purity and mildness.

At this point, Dove wasn't worrying about Ivory. For years, P&G had wanted a product like Dove, and they finally had it. It was in test-market in the US under the Oil of Olay name, and was doing well. Like Dove, Olay was not a soap, and it brought Dove's long reign of product superiority to an end. Lever were very concerned about what would happen when Olay arrived in Canada, as it must.

Lever decided to pre-empt the arrival of Olay by kick-starting Dove sales. This was easier said than done, because traditional methods (pricing and promotion) would hit the bottom line too hard. There was no product improvement in the wings, so attention shifted to advertising.

It so happened that Dove has close-to-neutral pH, while soaps are highly alkaline. Dove had shown this to dermatologists, with soap turning litmus paper dark, but they had never used such a "scientific" approach in consumer advertising. The team in Canada felt that litmus was just what they needed. There was a problem, however. The litmus test positioned Dove as *mild*. This was a strategic shift from "not drying," and it was right in Ivory's wheelhouse. Alarm bells went off.

Those who felt it was wrong to fight head on (this included the brass at the client and the agency head offices) were appalled. But the Canadian team decided to attack anyway. They launched the "Litmus" commercial, and a corresponding print ad. Four years later (with other advertising over time) Dove was up 73% in dollar sales, and Ivory had lost half its share. The Oil of Olay bar arrived some time later, but did not establish itself at a threatening level.[18]

Other examples of head on, or close to head on, attacks are the Pepsi Challenge, and Sunlight's "Go Ahead. Get Dirty." campaign against Tide.[19]

---

18 The full story is at www.cassies.ca. Dove won the Sustained Success Gold in Cassies III (1997).

19 Sunlight is also at www.cassies.ca, and was the Grand Prix winner in Cassies 99.

So how do you tell if you have what it takes to attack? Do not be side-tracked by "they got there first." Assess the situation on winnability.

This way of thinking is paramount in political races, but for some reason has not found its way into mainstream marketing. Ivory owned mildness, but the litmus story gave Dove a superb claim on that territory. Tide (seemingly) had cleaning locked up, but Sunlight refused to accept that they had the divine right of kings. Similar thinking drove Energizer and Pepsi.

If you are still troubled by the "me-too" bogeyman, let me try one last example. Imagine you were marketing insurance in the days when it was called Death Insurance. A competitor starts to call it Life Insurance. You wonder if you should do the same, but conclude that you shouldn't, because that would make you look like a me-too. You might as well take out some of your own insurance, and die.

Finally, having spent all this time on the issue, I have to close with a caveat. I'm not saying you should always attack head on (though, as you can no doubt tell, the high ground is the first place I think you should look.)

Staying the Course while Staying Fresh

This is broader than advertising, of course, but the question usually comes when deciding what to do with a campaign. Most of the chapters in the book touch on this in one form or another. There is also food for thought in the Crossover Notes at www.cassies.ca, from which the following is extracted.[20]

Let's start with a brand that is doing well—and you have to decide how to evolve the campaign. What might that entail? It helps to have an idea of what a "campaign" is.

---

20 See Crossover Notes #10. Conventional Wisdom—should it be challenged? #11. The Eureka Insight. #12. Changing the Goalposts. #13. Immediate vs. Long-Term Effect. #14. Refreshing a continuing campaign. #15. Baby with the Bathwater.

The following is not exhaustive, but it covers things to consider. It starts at the rigid end of the spectrum, and finishes at the most flexible:

- *Pool-out.* These are campaigns like "Who wants gum? I do. I do." Some regard this type of campaign as old-fashioned. Others, particularly those from the USP tradition, regard them fondly.
- *Hall of fame pool-out.* The pool-out can still deliver fabulously effective and creative advertising. The renowned example is the UK campaign for Hamlet cigars, which ran for twenty-odd years, and acquired folklore status.
- *Icons.* These can define a campaign (Maytag Repair Man, Marlboro Cowboy) or be a continuing property (Tony the Tiger, Pillsbury Doughboy). Michelin is trying to boost the Michelin Man, apparently having lost faith in the fabulous campaign: "Because so much is riding on your tires." Some see icons as passé, but I think it's a question of how it's done.
- **Spokes-people, and spokes-animals.** Dave Thomas, god rest his soul, would be a recent example, as would the Taco Bell Chihuahua. Campaigns with well-known personalities have been very successful in Quebec, e.g. the Pepsi and Listerine Grand Prix winners in Cassies I (1993) and II (1995).
- **Storytelling.** Campaigns built around continuing character(s) that we get to know. The Oxo campaign in the UK is perhaps the longest-running example. Quebec has had various examples.
- **Music-based.** Common in Soft Drinks, Cars, Fast Food, Beer. In packaged goods, becel's "young at heart" campaign would be an example.
- **Consistent "voice and attitude."** The benchmark was VW in the 60s. Executions ranged from serious to comical to ironic to dramatic. All had the Volkswagen voice and attitude. Nike is in this category.
- **Same message. Customized execution.** Dove "Litmus" was a minimalist demonstration, with haunting music, no voice over, no people, and the story in supers. Then came the opposite: women reacting riotously to the litmus test in a candid camera focus group. Then a talking head with the scientist who invented Dove. Then another demonstration. This was all held together by the promise of mildness, an element of surprise, and a straightforward brand character. The format varied completely, but the results were exceptional.

Note: there have been successful campaigns from *every point* on the spectrum. For this reason, it is not a good idea to think in terms of formats. Best practice is (1) define the issue (2) create the solution (3) let the campaign fall out of this.[21]

When a Campaign Stumbles

Sooner or later we are all in this situation. The pressures are extreme, but we must still solve the right problem. When Sanka first ran into trouble, it was being attacked by line extensions on all sides, and it tasted awful. It should have been no surprise that it was losing share— and that the solution (even if expensive) was to fix the product, and only then fix the advertising.[22]

That pill was too hard to swallow, and the brand went on a long and fruitless wander in the wilderness, looking for an advertising solution that wasn't there.

The difficult question is whether it is a momentary stutter which (if we were clairvoyant) we would solve with a minor fix. Or, is it a clue that something is going dangerously off the rails. Pressure can lead to snap (and wrong) judgments. The best answer comes from a blend of experience, judgment, intuition, vision, and research, applied to every facet of the marketing mix. That said, let's say that the problem is with the advertising. The next question becomes:

Are we looking at a problem of strategy, execution, or both?

This is a fork in the road. A successful long-running campaign may be jettisoned for the wrong reason, or you may hang on to a campaign that has run its course. It can be difficult to disentangle strategy from execution. Some suggestions:

---

21 I'm told that when the Pepsi Challenge was first shown to Pepsi executives in the US they refused to approve it, saying, "That's not Pepsi." Dove "Litmus" came under extreme pressure from client and agency head offices as being "Not Dove."

22 Before they launched "Go Ahead. Get Dirty." Lever bit the bullet and upgraded the Sunlight product, to make it competitive with Tide.

- *Dig deep into trends and tastes.* As explained in Listerine's 2002 Cassies case, "fighting bad breath" had been the high ground for as long as anyone could remember. But the tectonic plates were shifting towards the idea of a healthy mouth. Changes like this can be severely damaging to a brand's health. (Crest, as discussed earlier, is a case in point)
- *Re-examine the goalposts.* If they really haven't changed, then it's likely that you just have a short-term stutter to fix. (There can be big differences between the effectiveness of one execution and another, even when produced by the same people to the same strategy.)
- *Think through your definition of a campaign.* It may be that you can refresh the campaign by being more flexible. Clearnet (Cassies 2001) is a wonderful example of keeping a campaign fresh.
- *Think through your attitude to change.* It's broadly true that long-running campaigns—kept fresh and relevant—are great brand-builders. And it's sadly true that new people, wanting to make their mark, make change for change's sake. But once in a while, wholesale change is right.

Molson Canadian (Cassies I – 1993) was a niche player when it launched "What Beer's all About" in the late 80s. This reshaped the market, and Canadian eventually took over from Labatt Blue as #1. With this success, you would think they would keep the campaign going. But in the mid 90s, they realized that trends were shifting. So they launched the "I AM" campaign, described in Cassies III (1997). This then ran out of steam, and Canadian reincarnated again with "Joe's Rant" as described in Cassies 2001.

- *Go back to first principles.* Andy Macaulay discusses this in his chapter.

In Conclusion

I hope this has clarified the picture, without cluttering the landscape. Our next chapter is from a client with a gift for seeing things simply— Peter Elwood.

Bibliography

There are so many references that it is difficult to know what to include. I'll start with four books that I think everyone should read, and then list others.

Aaker, D., & Joachimsthaler, E. (2000). *Brand Leadership*. New York: The Free Press.

Bedbury, S. (2002). *A New Brand World: 8 Principles for Achieving Brand Leadership in the 21st Century*. New York: Viking.

Butterfield, L. ed. (2003). *AdValue: Twenty Ways that Advertising Works for Business*. Oxford: Butterworth Heinemann.

Steel, J. (1998). *Truth, Lies & Advertising: The Art of Account Planning*. NewYork: Wiley.

Baxter, M. (1999, July). "Advertising and Profitability: The Long-term Returns." *Admap*.

Biel, A. (1990, November). "Marketing Accountability: Strong Brand, High Spend-Tracking Relationships between the Marketing Mix and Brand Values."*Admap*.

Buzzel, R.D., & Gale, B.T. (1987). *PIMS Principles: Linking Strategy to Performance*. New York: Free Press.

Hillier, T. (1999, January). "Are you Profiting from Marketing?." *Admap*.

Lodish L., & Lubetkin B. (1992, February). "General Truths? Nine Key Findings from the IRI Test Data." *Admap*, 27(2).

Jones, J.P. (1986). *What's in a Name: Advertising and the Concept of Brands*. Lexington Mass.: Lexington Books.

Jones, J.P. (1995). *When Ads Work: New Proof that Advertising Triggers Sales*. New York: Lexington Books.

McDonald, C. (1992). *How Advertising Works: A Review of Current Thinking*. Oxfordshire, U.K.: NTC Publications.

www.cassies.ca

Overview: Chapter Two

David Ogilvy said, "Clients get the advertising they deserve." This has two meanings, according to the situation. On the positive side, it hails a client's immense motivational value. On the downside, it describes what happens when a client (often without realizing it) is part of the problem.

E. Peter Elwood is ideally positioned to speak to this. He had a stellar career with Unilever Canada, having been President of Lipton, and Lever Brothers, and VP of Marketing at both companies.

He challenged, and still challenges, conventional wisdom, and inspires this in others. This shows in the legacy of his brands, and in the people who worked for him. He had an influence, directly or from afar, on four major Cassies winners:

- Dove. Sustained Success in CASSIES III (1997).
- Sunlight. The Grand Prix in CASSIES 99.
- becel. Sustained Success in CASSIES 99.
- Lipton Chicken Noodle. Gold for Packaged Goods in CASSIES 2001.

From the agency side, he had the highest kudos of all—top people clamoured to work on his business.

He distills his thoughts here.

Chapter Two

So What Do You Deserve?

E. PETER ELWOOD

[Editor's Note: Peter gave these thoughts in a Q & A session.]

Q: We should probably start by clarifying who you have in mind as an audience for this conversation.

EPE: Well, in the broadest sense, I'm talking to anyone who's trying to build business by building brands—and that would include clients, agency people, promotions people, research people, the whole spectrum. But I guess like a good creative brief, we had better be focused. So my main audience is *clients*. Within clients, I think my remarks could be useful at any level, but I have in mind the people with the most influence on their brands—and that includes CEOs, who in my opinion have a tendency to walk away from this.[1]

Q: You mentioned brands. Can you comment on what brands are all about, and why they are so important?

EPE: There used to be a lot of categories where the product—the thing produced in the factory—had a performance advantage over competition. Dove was in this position for years because of its patented formula. Nowadays, this is increasingly rare. Products are easily duplicated, and quickly too. But a brand isn't a product. It's a set of hopes, expectations, and beliefs in the consumer's

---

1 To avoid having to say "marketing communication and promotional partners" we will use the word "agency" to embrace all disciplines

mind, and heart as well. Brands like this are the key to long-term business success. Now, we mustn't forget that a strong brand needs to be anchored to a good product, but the real competitive edge comes from the hopes, expectations and beliefs, and a lot of this comes from what you create through your agencies.

Q: When you first start working with an agency, what do you do?

EPE: The first thing is *to meet them*—in person, in a relaxed setting. To me, one of the astonishing things about this business is how many clients (especially senior clients) keep the agency at arm's length. I know there are impossible pressures on everybody's time, but if you think about the immense difference—to your company and to you personally—between having successful and unsuccessful brands, then surely it makes sense to build a relationship with the people creating the campaigns for those brands.

Q: When you meet with agency people, what do you have in mind?

EPE: The first is to define expectations. For example, do you want:

- business counsel
- marketing counsel
- communication counsel

A good client will accept all three, but the best place to focus is on communication issues.

Q: And other areas?

EPE: Getting to know your agency people very well:

- Their background—to see if it matches what you need.
- Their personalities and interests—so that you can get on each other's wavelength.
- Their strategic/marketing/communication skill—to see how much you will have to lead them, and how much they will be able to lead you.

- Their approach to the business—to see if working with you will enthuse them or (hopefully not) depress them.
- Their work. Show an interest—a genuine interest, in creative, strategic thinking, media innovation, whatever.

Q: You mentioned three levels of counsel that you could get from an agency. Have you run into the problem of getting advice and recommendations from people who are too junior?

EPE: It can happen, but not if you set up expectations properly. Suppose I'm wrestling with a tough business issue. There are senior agency people who've seen far more business and marketing situations than I have. So do my people ask their people for an agency POV in the old formal way? No. This creates dreadful wheel-spinning. Far better is to call up the person who can help you and find a congenial way to bounce ideas off each other.

Q: You make it sound simple, but what about hierarchy problems? Agencies would love more access to senior management, and any number of them get the message, "don't you dare go over my head" from their day-to-day clients. As a VP Marketing or CEO you had direct contact with the agency. How did you handle that internally?

EPE: I said earlier that you have to set up the right expectations with your agencies. It's also essential with your own people. My approach is pretty straightforward. I expect the marketing team to push for what is best for the brand. But I tell them that no one has the gift of second sight when it comes to knowing, for sure, what that is.

The point is that with people who really care, disagreement is *bound to happen*. Why are we so afraid of this? I love it when the sparks fly! Those sparks can light a fire under a brand. Of course, you have to pick your spots. I only get involved on critical issues. [See later for Peter's view on creative presentations.] It's also essential to involve the marketing team—either by making it a group effort, or by debriefing them immediately after the event.

Q: You seem to be describing the partnership model.

EPE: Yes. If you *live* it, it makes a tremendous difference.

- Share *all* knowledge. Loves and hates. Business needs. Organizational pitfalls. The realities of your firm.
- Share your SWOT thinking, consumer research, etc.
- Be accessible and available.
- Be a good listener.
- Don't expect the agency to be clairvoyant—I'm talking about the complaint where one client says to another "you would think they would have known that...."
- Help the agency use its resources well. Suppose the agency wants to show initiative? That's terrific. But what if they do it where you don't want it—let's say with pack designs for a relaunch, when you are happily handling this with someone else. It's like that awful feeling of getting a gift you don't want. Tell the agency (and your own people) ahead of time where you want them to focus, and also where you *don't*.

Q: What would you say to someone who thinks this is too open—that it's better to work on a more closed, need-to-know attitude?

EPE: [laughing] Well, the flip answer would be to say that I hope they are my competitors.

Look, all companies have their trade secrets, but very few are up there with Coke's secret formula. I think that people are pretty good when it comes to handling confidential information. Also, there's so much job turnover, on the client side and the agency side, that if things are going to leak, they are going to leak. But over and above that, the information is probably out of date or off-base anyway. In my entire career, I can't think of anything that I've heard through the grapevine that made much of a difference.

Q: So what does make a difference?

EPE: Attracting and motivating the smartest and best people—to your own firm, and as outside partners.

Q: But isn't this in the Mission Statement of every company?

EPE: Sure. The words are easy. But some companies are horrible at it. My point to a non-believer would be, "What type of environment do *you* find motivating?" I think it's what I'm describing.

Q: Speaking of environment, what are your thoughts on the day-to-day interaction with agencies?

EPE: The client should lead—with the agency's help, agreement and understanding—an efficient and motivated process for developing great work.

Q: Can you talk about what you mean by "lead"?

EPE: I believe unshakably that it is the client's job to lead—but not as a dictator. Volumes have been written about leadership. There are command-and-control models. There are teamwork models. Sooner or later there'll be a tough love model. There's no silver bullet. I developed my ideas from how a marketing group works best. If people are any good, they are positive, proactive, even pushy. I harness and encourage that energy, without stifling it. That's the leadership I'm talking about.

Q: You also mentioned "efficient and motivated."

EPE: If you say to creative people "I'm big on efficiency" their hearts sink, because that's a code-word for checklists and procedures. But a good client can strip out the wheel-spinning:

- Get early agreement from senior management on creative objectives, strategy and budgets.
- Have senior management *continuously involved* in the creative approval process.
- Stamp out those harrowing sequential creative presentations that start at the most junior level of the client.
- Do research only when uncertainty about the issue is large.

Q: This is very different from how some clients work. Can you
     develop these points a little?

EPE: Let's start with the first two. Everyone on the client side, at some
     point, has had the rug pulled by senior management. You and the
     agency do an enormous amount of work. You *think* management
     is on board because they've signed off on the strategy. Then, they
     see the work, and say, "this isn't what we agreed to?"

     Why does this happen?

     On the one hand, there's the largely fallacious notion that strate-
     gies are so clear that senior managers "know" what they are
     agreeing to. On the other, a lot of middle managers want to keep
     senior managers out of the tent. Added to this, a lot of senior peo-
     ple believe that they shouldn't sully their hands with something
     as lowly as "execution."
        As far as I'm concerned, the only way to make sure that top
     management "get it" is to make us part of the process. Then, we
     have to offer encouragement and guidance, without jumping into
     the driver's seat.

Q: What about presentations?

EPE: I can't think of anything more destructive and demotivating than
     the "juniors first" process. We only have ourselves to blame, in
     that the idea came out of firms like mine [Unilever] and our arch-
     enemy [P&G] in the 50s and 60s. On the surface, it seems like a
     good idea:

     • Advertising judgment (knowing what is likely to work and
       what isn't) is a mix of knowledge, experience and intuition.
     • It is *not* something we are born with. It has to be learned.
     • We need to train junior people to hone their judgment.

     But then came a hideous example of looking through the wrong
     end of the telescope.

Someone decided that if junior folk *just watched and listened,* they wouldn't learn anything. As it was explained to me, "It's a trial by fire. We force you to have a point of view, and we force you to go first, before you can see which way the wind is blowing.?

This is character-building stuff. But there's a devastating problem. When put to this test, most junior people raise "concerns." And once a concern has been sounded, you can't un-ring that bell. The agency then feels it has to respond. Battle lines get drawn. Before you know it, a comment by the most junior person in the room has sent the meeting careering off the track. And creative people are expected to find this motivating! Ideas are too fragile to be put through this "juniors first" wringer.

Q: So are you in favour of the "one meeting" approach?

A: This is one method. There's also the tissue session where ideas get explored, and at a fairly rough stage, before I would be brought in. The point is to avoid losing a great idea because of a clumsy process.

Q: And in the meeting itself?

A: I want the senior people to comment first, always constructively, of course. I will often throw in a positive comment to help set the tone, and then sit back. And if there are "concerns" let them come from the people with experience.

Q: This raises the question of research.

EPE: Whenever this topic comes up I always feel that people are grinding their axes. Here's how I look at it:

- I start from the point that everyone involved—client, agency and researchers—has to want what's best for the brand.
- I accept that there will be different beliefs about that.
- I accept that research can be useful, but *not* that it is infallible.

- Equally, I accept that individual judgments are fallible.
- I'm very interested in research that stimulates ideas and insights.
- I'm more guarded about research that claims to be predictive—for the simple reason that these predictions, in my experience, bat at well less than 1.000.
- There's also something deeper. Most research, by its nature, draws on past experience. But what if you are trying to break new ground? To paraphrase a quote: if you rely on research, you are driving into the future while looking in the rear-view mirror.

That's why, as I said earlier, if the issue is a big one, and research can help, I will happily use it. But the rest of the time, I prefer to rely on the experience and judgment of the team—which includes me, of course!

Q: What about research being used to help reassure people up the line?

EPE: [laughs] Ah yes—research as crutch. It happens, and it's a pity. It's a long way from the trail-blazing image this business has of itself. Far more important is to engender courage in your people and your agency. For example:

- Encouraging and approving advertising that breaks the tried and true rules. There are no rules, after all.
- Not being knocked off-stride if qualitative research throws up a few negative responses along with the positive ones. You can't be all things to all people.
- Not running scared if your advertising will offend a few people. (Aside: We live in a world with riots outside G-7 meetings, and misdeeds on the Enron scale, and yet we run for cover if we shock some delicate soul in suburbia.)
- Accepting the advice of agency partners—especially in the face of naysayers.

Q: What about convincing international management that Canada should do its own thing?

EPE: This can be a tough one. The argument that Canada is different from the US can be difficult to win—especially with Americans. It helps, of course, if you have a track record of success. And research may add something. Failing that, you can always suggest that Canada is the ideal place to try something new. If it succeeds, great. If not, nobody important will notice.

[Editor's note: Peter approved Dove "Litmus" in the face of intense international pressure not to. See Chapter 1.]

Q: How do you handle it when the creative is not doing the job?

EPE: There are a couple of answers. If it's at the creative presentation:

- Be straightforward, candid and honest.
- Be positive. Never switch into a prosecutorial mode.
- Explain what's on your mind in plain English.
- Listen.
- Do not try to write copy or display your divine instinct for art direction. Don't say "I'm not trying to write copy" or "I'm not trying to be an Art Director." Clients have many talents, but writing and art direction are not amongst them.
- Make sure the agency is crystal clear on the next steps.

Q: And the other answer?

EPE: This one is tougher. It's when the work has been produced, with high hopes, but it has bombed. Who said "Principles aren't principles until you have to pay the price." This is when you learn something about the people around you. But more importantly, you learn something about yourself. My thinking on this:

- Nothing ventured, nothing gained. If you can't bounce back from failure, you should not be in this business.
- Don't lay blame—it won't help. If you want to criticize anyone, criticize yourself. Show leadership, and take responsibility.
- Learn, but do not go into your shell next time.
- Stick to your principles.

Q: How about when things have gone well?

EPE: Compliment your agency immediately and often.

Q: Any final thoughts?

EPE: Never give up. There will always be another opportunity to do great work.

Overview: Chapter Three

Before we get to Andy Macaulay's discussion of Advertising Strategy, we need to put it in context. Here's his favourite definition of a successful brand:

> A promise for which there is no acceptable substitute.

Like other definitions (see Chapter 1) this is all about the perceptions and reality that ring true to the customer—in a way that no other brand does.

Advertising Strategy is critical to this, though in a sense it is a misnomer. The thinking that Andy has in mind goes far wider and deeper than advertising, even with its expanded definition of persuasive communication.

He also touches on the type of brainpower you need for great strategy, and the need for a positive, free, and frank environment.

In Andy's words, whether you think in terms of Brand Essence, or Positioning, or one of the many concepts in use today, great brands find the truths that allow them to deliver on their promise.

Chapter Three

Advertising Strategy Development

ANDY MACAULAY

Introduction

Given the explosion of terminology in our business, we should probably start with a definition of advertising:

> From the dictionary: To call public attention by emphasizing desirable qualities so as to arouse a desire to buy or patronize.

> Or, from a standup comic: a technique that makes you believe you've longed all your life for something you've never heard of before.

The thing that these two definitions have in common is emotion—and "arousing a desire" or "longing" are achieved by the alchemy of advertising strategy and its execution. That's right, it's alchemy and not mathematics. The end goal is to create desire, not awareness, or even understanding. Desire lives in the heart (if not somewhere south of there) and not in the head. So good strategy development isn't about a string of logic. It's as intuitive and creative as advertising itself. However, as with any form of chemistry, repeatable success requires some processes and guidelines. It is those that we'll try to document here.

What Is Strategy?

Every profession invents its own unique lexicon. This serves two purposes: it allows professionals to show how smart they are, and it allows insiders inside to keep outsiders outside.

Every once in a while comes a word so powerful that it shows up in every lexicon. Strategy is such a word, and in our business it is used to make everything sound more legitimate. "Strategic" is smart and well thought-out, while "tactical" or "executional" are somehow seen as random, even knee-jerk, and of little long-term value.

Nothing could be further from the truth. We should not forget that customers only see the executions that bring strategy to life. In that sense (despite the fact that it is sometimes put well down in the pecking order) execution can be at least as important as strategy.

Given the fetishism over strategy, it needs a tight definition. In our business we are usually dealing with competitive situations, and strategy is a well-founded, systematic (sometimes elaborate) plan of action:

a) Conceived to achieve a significant goal.
b) Achieved by applying strength, often ingeniously, against weakness.

This second point can be overlooked or misjudged, especially if "strength" and "weakness" don't neatly line up. For example, suppose two football teams face off in a cup final. Your team has a powerful passing game. The other a superb pass defence. As the offensive strategist, do you "go with what got us here" and rely on your passing game, or look for another strategy?

Our business is full of examples. The solution relies on an alert and dispassionate (not prejudiced or preconceived) assessment of what is truly a strength and what is truly a weakness.

Words, Words, Words...

This chapter is about Advertising Strategy, but because they overlap, it applies equally to Brand Essence (and its siblings), Positioning, and Creative Strategy.

Brand Essence is one of those concepts that is felt, rather than driven by dry logic. Not all companies use it, but many do, including us at ZiG. Finding the deep meaning of a brand pays handsome rewards, but is not always easy, as these quotes show:

Gord Shank gave us ten words and said, "This is Levi's." They were words like authenticity, irreverence, honesty, originality, timeless, youthful, and so on. That was it.[1]

We use ... a concise articulation of the brand's core meanings ... the very essence of the brand distilled. One sheet of paper. Three character attributes. No more than six lines. It's one of the most exhausting and creative things we do with our clients.[2]

I want you to conduct a Big Dig. I want you to dig deeply into everything that has ever been written, felt, said, or thought about coffee.[3]

Positioning is still much in use, as the territory the brand wants to own in the customer's mind. It is still useful, but given that the idea is to be focused, it's sad that many positionings are so complex. They suffer from "all things to all people" disease, or its cousin, "nothing compelling to anybody."

Creative Strategy defines the story the brand is to tell, sometimes referred to as the WHAT, to distinguish it from the actual execution, which is the HOW. David Rutherford discusses the history behind this in Chapter 1.

Beliefs About Strategy

There are different schools of thought about how long an advertising (or creative) strategy should stay in place. Some people believe that once it has been set, and been successful in the market, it should be changed only in the face of *force majeure*—such as a major change in market conditions. They point to horror stories of brands changing strategy too often. They also want to head off a dangerous practice— strategies that get changed at the whim of new people on a brand. The

---

1 Brian Harrod, referring to the relationship he and Ian Mirlin had with Levi's.
2 Dom Caruso, then at MacLaren McCann.
3 Scott Bedbury, taking the first step to cracking the Starbucks genetic code.

other school is more flexible, with their own horror stories of brands that held on to old beliefs when they should have changed them.

This is a clash between "if it ain't broke don't fix it" and "if it ain't broke, change it before it breaks." Ideally, they should take second place to the higher goal—*to do what's best for the brand.*

In terms of process, strategy development is *not* a point-in-time operation. It's not even a line of points in time. It's a loop. For you, it will have a beginning and an end. But in most cases the brand existed before you, and it will exist after. Respect this. Also, make sure that "the strategy" does not acquire an undeserved halo. There is a tendency to worship it, rather than treating it as a means to an end. A strategy should be like the referee at a hockey game, quietly and skillfully guiding the effort, but allowing the beauty of the game (in our case the brand) to engage the audience.

In a world of integrated communication, strategy must also recognize what advertising can and cannot do. One of its most compelling roles is to build emotional brand values. However, with our widespread population, and the size of budgets, we need to be realistic about what can be delivered. It may be necessary (with all but really big-budget brands) to achieve brand objectives over the long term.

Finally, a quote from Ed McCabe of Scali, McCabe and Sloves, to support why we must get the advertising strategy correct:

> Advertising is the last legal source of unfair competitive advantage.

A Strategy System

Strategic thinking is influenced by how well or badly a brand is doing. Ideally, this should not be the case, and we should interrogate the brand from square one, always looking for ways to sharpen, evolve, change or confirm existing thinking. The starting point is the loop we referred to earlier. It's a series of four questions:

1. Where are we now, and why?
2. Where do we want to be?
3. How should we get there?
4. Are we getting there? (Then back to Question 1.)[4]

---

4 These questions came from Stephen King of JWT in the UK. There were originally five, with "why" separated out. Lisa Elder has a similar list in her chapter.

First, let's look at the type of brainpower best suited to strategy work. Part of strategic thinking is linear and logical. For example, although we glorify the heroic exceptions, most of the battles in human history have been won by the army with more troops and better weapons. This means that you need the sort of mind that can, in Ross Johnson's words, recognize a blinding glimpse of the obvious, and not be diverted by irrelevancies.

On the other hand, you often don't have the advantage of brute strength. Then, you need a mind that is lateral, even subversive, as when Wolfe had his soldiers scale those supposedly unclimbable cliffs. *What most see as irrelevant or impossible, the lateral thinkers see as opportunity.*

You need people who love the Big Dig. We are under relentless pressure to come up with snap answers—even though history shows that such answers are often wrong. The Big Dig people want to explore everything, and they are invaluable. So are people with an instinct for human nature. And people with an eye to what's possible. Blue-sky brilliance can trigger wonderful ideas, but someone has to assess if those ideas will work.

Are there superhumans who combine these characteristics? Very few. That's why it's best to have a mix of abilities on the client/agency/ researcher team—and for clients to realize the tremendous leverage they have (for good or, sadly, sometimes for bad) depending on the environment they create. That said, the lead role for advertising strategy generally falls to the agency—to the planning and account management people, with some input from the creative group. Let's turn now to the four questions that guide how they can go about the job.

QUESTION 1—WHERE ARE WE NOW AND WHY?

For most brands, success or failure depends on the interplay of four forces:

- *Societal/economic trends.* Examples might be the love or fear of technology, healthy eating, women working outside the home, higher or lower interest rates, optimism or pessimism about the future, and so on.
- *Competitive pressure.*
- *The customer mindset.* Everything from their impression of one brand versus another, to their readiness to buy at all, to their deeper hopes and fears, to their desire for change versus the status quo, and so on.
- *Your brand's strengths and weaknesses.* These will be perceived (in the mind) and real (objectively verifiable, whether the customer has picked up on them or not). Where appropriate, this area also includes the relationship with the retail trade, distribution issues, and similar factors.

Like a ping-pong ball assaulted by jets of water, your brand may dance around giving no clear picture of what is driving it. You have to examine all the forces. At this stage you should probably not come to firm conclusions (you may be jumping to wrong ones) but you should develop hypotheses. Many people do a SWOT analysis. This can work well, provided you are honest in your assessment.

Another approach is a sequence of questions that David Rutherford likes to ask:

- Who's up? Who's down? Who's chugging along?
- Who's got the best marketing mix?
- Who's winning the battle for the mind and heart?
- How does this explain the market results?
- What's the opportunity that we have all been missing?

The first question requires you to look at long-term data. Get the trends for the past three, five, or (depending on the category) even ten years.

For the marketing mix you need to look at product, packaging, pricing, etc. on all key brands—especially those that are doing well. You analyze blind tests, satisfaction surveys, customer complaints (a rich source), the price the consumer actually pays, spending levels, and so on. You also factor in societal and economic trends.

The battle for the customer's mind and heart is the crucial part, so you look at it separately. Brands *try* to get their hooks into the customer, but they don't always succeed. Go well beyond simply looking at competitive effort, and work out what is actually getting through. This is where image studies, tracking studies, etc. are useful. Qualitative studies are also a goldmine.

All the time, look for eurekas. When Clearnet launched, the obvious thing was to slog it out with Bell Mobility and Rogers using price and promotion. They didn't. They anchored the brand to the visionary thought that "the future is friendly." Just three years after the launch, Telus bought Clearnet for $6.6 billion.[5]

Be especially alert when you find a loose end.[6] The repositioning of Johnson's Baby Shampoo against adults was the classic example of this:

- JBS was a baby product, through and through.
- It was a significant blind test loser to the adult shampoos.
- The colour, the thin texture, the perfume, the JBS name, the packaging, the advertising, the "no more tears" slogan, and the halo of the Johnson image were all "wrong" for adults.
- Meanwhile, a major shift was starting in haircare—away from the heavily coiffed look—towards washing hair every day.
- The positioning stretch between "baby" and "adult" was huge, and easy to reject or overlook.
- Even so, some brilliant soul(s) realized that JBS's gentleness could support "wash your hair everyday" with adults.
- This went to market, and JBS went to #1.[7]

II. QUESTION 2—WHERE DO WE WANT TO BE?

This is where advertising strategy connects to the overall business strategy.

---

5 For the full story, see www.cassies.ca

6 Loose ends can lead to a great discovery. Remember the *Hound of the Baskervilles.* "But Holmes," Dr. Watson replied, "none of the neighbors said anything about hearing a dog barking." "Precisely," the detective answered. "And don't you find that peculiar?"

7 This is a particularly interesting example of "strength against weakness" because the JBS product was in fact "weak" but by a twist of fate this was its strength.

Virtually all companies express the Marketing Objective in the hard numbers of sales, share, and profit. Some additionally express "softer" objectives such as leadership, or growth, or owning certain territory in the customer's mind.

Often, the numbers are driven by forces outside the brand—such as quarterly earnings. This can lead to goals that are, to say the least, ambitious. *It's up to the person setting the business strategy to ensure that advertising is allocated enough money to achieve what it needs to do, and get the brand where it needs to go.*

This does not always happen, of course, and the consequences need careful handling. Someone who says in good faith that the objectives are too ambitious can quickly, and unjustly, be branded a naysayer. However, consumers are blissfully unaware of what is going on in the boardroom, and they will not buy the brand just because the annual plan says that they will. As with everything to do with strategy, free and frank discussion between the client and the agency is best.

Independent of this issue, there is the question of what the brand should stand for in the customer's mind and heart. This brings us to the art of finding the truth. Or, more appropriately, the truths. Whether you think in terms of Brand Essence, or Positioning, or one of the many concepts in use today, great brands are based on a confluence of three things:

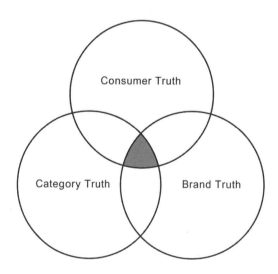

Sometimes, these are self-evident. But sometimes—this is the thrill of strategy—you suddenly reimagine what's possible. Such insights can leave the feeling, "Aha, I already knew that." But no one has quite seen things that way before.[8]

Let's look at each of these areas in turn, and how they come together:

a) *Consumer Truths*

Two things are needed here. First, you must decide (or confirm) who the "best customer" is. This includes assessing the relative value of current versus potential users, bringing into play such things as the time, effort and investment needed to keep someone loyal versus converting someone new.

Then, you isolate what it is about their attitudes, beliefs, and behaviours that can, or will, make them want your brand. You dig for powerful, deep motivations. As an example, there are drivers who want to get from A to B, and those who love to drive. Strategists on VW mined the latter group and found an overarching need for *control.* This underpins the "Drivers Wanted" campaign. Clearnet, as noted, turned discomfort about technology into an uplifting attitude towards the future.

b) *Category Truths*

You ask devastatingly simple questions. Why does the category exist? What needs does it meet? What would consumers do if the category were taken away?

Here's a story that I was given, as they say, by reliable sources. It has not often been told, because it starts with a failure. Twenty or so years ago, two trends were emerging—women were increasingly working outside the home, and people were thinking more and more about healthy eating. At that time, the dominant soup usage was at lunchtime when kids came home from school and Mom was there to greet them. Campbell's were concerned that this prime occasion was going to decline. But those dangerous trends were also creating opportunity.

---

8 Don't confuse insights with facts. In the JBS story, it was a fact to say "adults are looking for ways to wash their hair every day." It was an *insight* to link this to JBS.

Soup is nutritious. It's quick and easy to prepare. You can eat it any-time. So Campbell's launched a TV campaign positioning their soup as a healthy, active, vigorous solution to the increasing pace of life.

They put the advertising through their research protocol, and it cleared all the hurdles. It was launched with high hopes. And it did nothing for the business.

There was a postmortem, with in-depth research (something they had not felt the need for first time around). The researcher came back with one of those how-did-we-miss-it insights. Soup is unalterably s-l-o-w, and the advertising was telling people that it's fast."[9] The agency developed fresh advertising to reflect this truth, and this new campaign built the business.

c) Brand Truths

Who owns what? What could they own? If a brand is "a promise for which there is no acceptable substitute" is your brand living up to it? Are you exploiting functional and emotional benefits, and values. In a world where products, functionally, are often close to parity, how will you be *distinctive?* One of the UK agencies describes the search like this:

> We interrogate the product until it confesses its strength

Procter & Gamble put it more bluntly:

> We have to decide what it is, real and perceived, that will convince the target to buy our brand in preference to the competition.

Like other truths, Brand Truths may be waiting to be discovered. We worked on a brand with a powerful truth at its core, in a market where brand truths are uncommon. The Sleeman family began brewing beer in 1834 in Guelph, Ontario, and did so until forced to close the brewery in the 30s due to a prohibition violation. When John Sleeman reopened the brewery in the 80s, he looked to that truth—a heritage of brewing

---

9   The researcher was Peter Hume, who got this wonderful thought from a consumer: "Soup is cuddletum food."

quality beer from a time when the beer was more important than the marketing—and it guided every marketing decision he made. Each aspect of the story (the bottle, the crest, locating the brewery in Guelph) amplified this truth and made Sleeman Cream Ale the fastest growing premium beer in Ontario at launch, and we helped them reattain that in summer 2002.

There is also the story of David Ogilvy and Dove. He asked for a tour of the factory. It was boring—nothing to go on. Then he was told that Dove contained stearic acid, or some such dreadful thing. His antennae flickered. "What is that?" "Oh," said the technical guy, "You probably know it as the main ingredient in cold cream."

From this came the long-running Dove claim. And as a side note on managing brand truth over time, the claim itself has evolved. Dove launched when cold cream was the leading cleanser. As women's preferences changed, the claim morphed from ¼ cold cream to ¼ cleansing cream to ¼ moisturizing cream.

d) Bringing It All Together

You are hunting for the confluence of the three truths—consumer, category, and brand—because this is the heart of advertising strategy. Using the Campbell's story as an example, let's look at how this could have uncovered the miscue. In terms of the key thoughts, our diagram would look like this:

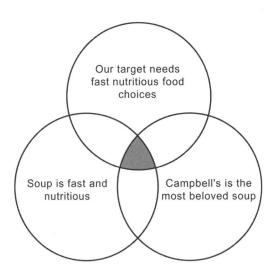

At this point (admittedly now with the benefit of hindsight) alarm bells would have gone off. Two of the three truths are fine, but the idea that soup is fast would at least have raised an eyebrow. Compare this to what was discovered after the in-depth interviewing:

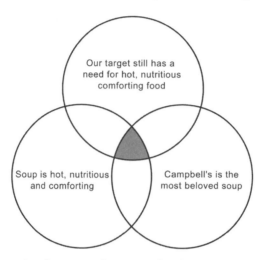

This time there is a harmony between the three truths, and this is very important. Here is a more recent ZiG example, for breast cancer.

Over the years there have been any number of attempts to get women to take charge of their own health. The difficulty is that all this effort, though logically valid, and utterly well-motivated, scares some women into denial. This allowed us to develop the following truths:

- Consumer Truth.   Fear-mongering PSA's cause people to disengage because they don't want to contemplate their own vulnerability.
- Category Truth.   Women under 40 don't worry about breast cancer but they should.
- Brand Truth.   Rethink Breast Cancer wants to replace fear with facts to change the way people think about Breast Cancer.

This led to the commercial illustrated. The objective was for women to see the issue in a new (non-threatening) way, and to go to the website for factual information.

Learn the Facts about Breast Cancer :30

1. Two guys chat, staring at each other's womanly breasts.

2. Guy on the bed bouncing up and down. He admires his breasts.

3. Guy takes a Polaroid photograph of his breasts.

4. If men had breasts, they'd really appreciate them.

5. Guy washing car. We cut as he's about to spray the water at his breasts.

6. Learn the facts about breast cancer.

e) *Capturing the Essential Thinking*

At this point, you may have more than one possibility for the brand. Some, based on experience and judgment, will have more potential than others. You have to capture them in a way that will be clear to the rest of the team. Different strategists and planners do it in different ways, but these are the principles:

- Use simple, evocative words to show the role of the brand in people's lives.[10]
- Identify if this is a continuation/evolution, or a major change.
- Watch the balance of rational versus emotional. (The emotional approach is almost always more powerful than we, with our business mindset, realize.)
- Don't use jargon, acronyms or gobbledygook. It is a major turnoff, especially to creative people, and it helps hide inferior thinking.

QUESTION 3—HOW SHOULD WE GET THERE?

From the nuggets of truth, we must determine what message could be delivered by what means and at what time to cause the chosen customer to think, feel, or do what we want them to, in order to get the brand to where we want it to be. Whew!

a) *Every Point of Contact*

This idea comes up throughout this book. At ZiG, our starting point is what we call Moments of Truth.[11] To explain this, I need to provide a little context. Brands are built experientially these days. With the fragmentation of media, and the increasing numbers of places to buy, the exposure to brands and their messages has increased exponentially. One way to start the strategy discussion is to analyze all the potential moments of interaction between the brand and its chosen

---

10 Pictures, video-clips, sound effects—anything that appeals to the five senses—are also sometimes used.

11 Authors were reticent about mentioning their companies, but as Editor I asked them not to be shy—so that the learning can be as concrete as possible.

customers. Some of those Moments will have more meaning than others (a radio spot for a beer in the morning news will have less impact than an outdoor ad in front of a bar, for example) and figuring out which Moments to own is a key step in strategy development. The logic is that *a moment of heightened relevance* is better than a moment when you merely reach your audience.

Note that this approach looks not only for *when* the moment is, but also for *what's going on*. This helps trigger insights.

Moments of Truth also reflect the world of integrated communications, because they reveal all the different points of interception. What remains is to figure out what moments should be targeted using what form of communication, and with what message content.[12]

Here too, you have to think carefully about budget, to ensure that the goals are achievable. Conceiving a strategy that is lofty and emotional when all you have is money for shelf-talkers doesn't make a lot of sense.

b) The Creative Strategy

After the "truths" are pinned down (or sometimes while this is being done) most approaches call for a written Creative Strategy. The original format was laid down by the packaged goods companies about fifty years ago. As noted earlier, its function is to specify WHAT a brand will say, rather that HOW it will say it. This type of Creative Strategy lays out the agreed thinking, often in considerable detail. There are various approaches, but they tend to have similar ingredients. They work well when used with insight and empathy. Let's look at an example, by kind permission of the Ontario Lottery & Gaming Corporation and Bensimon•Byrne. The brand was Pro•Line, the campaign was a Cassies winner in 2002 and 2003, and the resulting advertising is at www.cassies.ca.

---

12 Discussed in detail in Chapters 9 and 10.

Why are we advertising?
Over the past few years Pro•Line has seen a slow decline in sales, attributed to a decline in players, specifically men aged 18 to 24. The primary goal is to bring in new 18 to 24-year-old users, while maintaining the core group of users.

What do we want the advertising to do?
Primary: Encourage wagering on Pro•Line among new, younger players.
Secondary: Continue momentum with current users.

How will it achieve this?
Convince sports fans that they could win money betting on sports with Pro•Line.

Who are we talking to and what do we know that will help?
> **Primary Target—New Users:** Males aged 18–24. They are sports fans to varying degrees and tend to wager with friends or in office pools, but have not yet made the leap to Pro•Line.
> **Secondary Target—Core Group/Current Users:** Heavy male skew, aged 25–34. 50–55% are graduates of college or higher. Mixture of white and blue collar. Feel they know sports—playing Pro•Line is a calculated gamble for them. They expect that they will win.
> **Bond to Create:** For new users, to convey the fact that extensive sport knowledge is NOT needed to play and win with Pro•Line.
> **Barrier to Overcome:** You have to be a sports expert to win on Pro•Line.

What's the main thought the advertising should get across?
You can win money betting on sports with Pro•Line.

Support
The unpredictable nature of sports.

Tone and Manner
Smart, provocative and funny. Convey the excitement associated with sports.

Executional Mandatories
- 2 x :30 second spots—One hockey, one football
- Timing: Start of each season, to tap in to the excitement
- Pro•Line logo
- OLGC logo must appear for a minimum of 1.8 seconds

Why are we advertising? (see opposite.)
This is a clear statement in plain English. There are two goals, which is not uncommon. Importantly, they are put in a definite hierarchy—in this case with new users being the more important.

What do we want the advertising to do?
This is consistent with the opening statement, thus maintaining focus.

How will it achieve this?
Responds to the question in the previous section, still maintaining focus.

Who are we talking to and what do we know that will help?
    Primary Target—New Users:
    Secondary Target—Core Group/Current Users:
    These sections follow the hierarchy in the opening statement, and this keeps the brief consistent.
    Bond to Create:
    Barrier to Overcome:
    These capture the insight that drove the campaign. It is a great example of "seeing what is not there." Conventional thinking said that you had to know sports to win. But because sport is unpredictable, this isn't true. This was particularly motivating with the new users.

What's the main thought the advertising should get across?
A KISS statement in plain English.

Support
Brands, and their advertising, must be distinctive. Here, the distinctiveness is not in the product. It is in the lives of the audience. This is important, because the tendency is to think that the reason why has to come from the product (Contac and its tiny little time pills). This thinking is too narrow.

Tone and Manner
The descriptors hang together. No oxymorons like "aggressive yet empathetic."

Executional Mandatories
Simple and pragmatic. Not a demotivating laundry list of do's and don'ts.

It's important to know, however, that some clients prefer to stay at 40,000 feet. This is what Gordon Shanks of Levi's did with his "ten words," and it is what Scott Bedbury insists on. He believes that if direction is too definitive it *restricts* the chances of finding the truly breakthrough solution. Here is the "creative strategy" he wrote to the agency soon after he arrived at Nike. The company was at a turning point, and he wanted the agency to envision the new way forward: [13]

> Nike is about to become a significant network television advertiser. We will spend nearly three times what we spent on "Revolution" in the fall of 1988. This is a turning point for a company that not long ago spoke to its customers at track meets from the tailgate of a station wagon. This cannot just be a narrow look back at where we have been.
>
> We should be proud of our heritage, but we must also recognize that the appeal of "Hayward Field" [a Nike commercial with somber shots of an empty, lonely, rain-slicked track] is narrow and potentially alienating to those who are not great athletes. We need to grow this brand beyond its purist core....
>
> We have to stop talking just to ourselves. It's time to widen the access point. We need to capture a more complete spectrum of the rewards for sports and fitness. We achieved this with "Revolution." [A much more inclusive Nike commercial.] Now we need to take the next step.

Bedbury is justifiably proud that "Just do it" came in response to this.

There is something special at the heart of good strategy. Although it will always be connected to the Key Consumer Benefit it is not always the benefit itself. It may be an insight into how to arouse the "longing and desire" we talked about earlier. It may be an insight into dramatizing the problem or the solution. It may be a unique way of portraying a point of difference.[14]

---

13 The extract is from *A New Brand World,* and there is more on these philosophical differences in Arthur Fleischmann's chapter.

14 This is related to distinctiveness. Many people say "our benefit has to be unique" but a lot of market leaders are built on the category benefit. This is discussed in "Where Does Distinctiveness Come From" in the Appendix to Chapter 1.

At ZiG we call this "the shout." If you were at a party, and had to say one thing quickly and succinctly to your customer—to get them to change their thoughts, feelings, or actions—what would it be? Writing "the shout" is tough. You must do four things at once:

- Be clear.
- Be single-minded.
- Be motivating (to both the creative team and the end consumer).
- Be right.

The box on the next page has a Cassies winner to illustrate this. The story started when the Canadian Egg Marketing Agency hired Roche Macaulay & Partners to reverse a seventeen-year per capita decline in egg consumption. In situations like this you will usually come up with a number of options. When making choices, look for the insights (and resulting "shouts") that have the power to surprise and motivate.

c) Research into Creative Strategy

On occasion, the "three truths" come together so harmoniously that agency and client know they have the right answer. But often, there are choices to be made, and judgment alone is not felt to be enough. This chapter is not about research technique. That, in itself, could take up a book. Some thoughts, however.

The planner's view, in general, is that research is invaluable at the searching and hypothesizing stage. There is less enthusiasm for "researching to find the right strategy."

Some clients (and researchers) find this lack of enthusiasm troubling. It crosses their mind that planners are not prepared to have their thinking put to the test and it's easy to see why that thought occurs. I remember how unsympathetic some planners were, especially those with children, when teachers were up in arms about being tested.

"Where Do We Want to Be"—The Egg Story

Fears of cholesterol and fat were restricting egg consumption in Canada. We asked "Where Are We Now" and noted that eggs had kept a low profile. Yes, there had been an attempt through PR to convince people that cholesterol in the egg does not equate to dangerous levels of cholesterol in the bloodstream. But it was a losing battle. We had to deal with this. The question was how?

We considered (briefly) the low profile approach—because it can be a mistake to stir up a hornet's nest. But history told us that this was a losing strategy. We looked at a head-on attack, but reasoned that advertising didn't have the credibility to combat what friends, neighbours, doctors, and the media were saying. We concluded that the "side door" had to be the way in.

Even then, there was the question of how. There are many truths about eggs: they're versatile, convenient, tasty, and nutritious. Could any of these combat cholesterol and fat? We began by standing in grocery aisles[15] and asking egg buyers: "What are the first five words you associate with eggs." Not one of the first 20 people said "natural."

This is another example of "seeing what is not there." We realized that we were onto something and asked the next 20 people, "Do you believe eggs are natural?" The answer was overwhelmingly yes. Subsequent qualitative research proved the point and led to the insight that drove the campaign:

Eggs are natural, and nature doesn't make unhealthy food.

Note how this (far more than versatility, convenience, taste, and nutrition) uses "strength against weakness." We had enlisted nature to our cause!

This insight became the "shout," and led to a gritty down-to-earth campaign with real egg farmers. One year later, per capita egg consumption had increased by 7%—an astonishing turnaround in a market that had been sinking like an ailing battleship.

---

15 Note *where* this happened, and see similar advice in Lisa Elder's chapter.

But this is not why we have the reservations. The pure and simple fact is that "strategy" is incredibly difficult to research validly.

First, there is the unsolvable Catch-22, that if you research strategy based on plain words (to remove selling bias) consumers very likely don't grasp the full implications of what is being said. But, if you use "selling" language or (horror of horrors) pictures or video, some say you are not testing strategy, but execution.

Then there is the debate over whether consumers can predict their future behaviour. You will see different stances on this question, but as planners we are guided by our experience. No methodology has risen to the top.

This is not to say that strategic research is inherently invalid. But it is a plea to use research wisely. As Lisa Elder says, quoting David Ogilvy, "They use research as a drunkard uses a lamppost—not for illumination but for support." This is not the way to great strategy.

d) Relating Positioning to Creative Strategy

These concepts overlap, but once in a while you have to pull them apart. What do you do, for example, if you have "Positioning" and "Creative Strategy" and both have sections for the audience, the benefit, and the reason why? In this situation, it's important *not* to use different language just for the sake of change. Here's why.

Positioning is the more far-reaching concept, and applies to the whole marketing mix. Creative Strategy is a subset of Positioning. It deals with what the brand will say, to drive home the Positioning, as vividly and convincingly as possible. Given this, you should *expect* the two statements to have language in common. Many packaged goods brands have worked in this way, very happily, for years. For example, a Duracell Positioning document might identify the key benefit as "long lasting" and the Creative Strategy would pick up that language identically.

But what's so wrong with a bit of wordsmithing? Here's what goes wrong. Suppose the Positioning calls for *trust* and in the Creative Strategy you finesse that into *confidence*. These are similar, but they are not the same. What you have done, in effect, is alter the Positioning with no justification.[16]

---

16 Imagine you worked on Nike and, for a change of pace, changed "authentic athletic performance" into some other set of words. It's unthinkable.

All of this refers to the situation where the Positioning is single-minded (or at least highly focused) and the creative task is "to drive the positioning home." There are, of course, other scenarios. For example, some Positioning Statements have several benefits.[17] Creative can't talk about everything, so the Creative Strategy selects the area to focus. The Eggs case would be an example of this.[18]

Alternatively, you may want to change behaviour. This is illustrated by UK milk. The Positioning was half a page long, but the Creative Strategy was based on exhorting Britons to drink more of the stuff. This led to the legendary campaign "Drinka Pinta Milka Day."

e) Multiple Benefits versus Single-Mindedness and Focus

Advertising Strategy, in a broad sense, embraces all channels of communication, and these work differently. For example, Direct Marketing and Interactive work very comfortably with multiple benefits. This is not the case with general advertising, such as broadcast, print, outdoor, etc.

From everyday life, we know that if something is complicated it is harder to grasp. We've all walked out of presentations that covered too much, totally bewildered. We've all done research with overstocked ads. Usually, not much gets through, although once in a while a multi-benefit approach works.[19]

This means that the Creative Strategy for general advertising has to be focused.

Why is it, then, that there is so much pressure (usually from clients) to force in additional benefits? We know the answer. With such pressure to deliver results, it is impossibly hard to leave things out. This issue has been around a long time, so it's doubtful that a few words can transform things, but the following may help:

---

17 Some believe that Positioning should be single-minded. See more in Chapter 1.
18 Another is the famous "Got Milk" campaign in the US. Milk has many benefits, but the Creative Strategy was based on two words: *milk deprivation*.
19 Vick's "night time, sniffling, sneezing, coughing, aching, stuffy-head, fever, so you can rest and have a good morning" campaign would be an example. But here, there is an ingenious idea that bundles the benefits together.

- Ask the major research companies what the track record is for advertising that is simple and focused, as compared to multi-benefit.
- Also ask them, "If you focus on one benefit, do other benefits come along for the ride, even though you don't talk about them?" The answer is yes, because of what David Rutherford has called slip-streaming.[20]

There's another scenario, too. Time was when advertising found a single benefit and stuck to it—assuming it was working—year after year. This will still be valid for some brands, but nowadays we have to think about what Alan Middleton calls "longitudinal" management (i.e. over time) in his chapter.

Consider Levi's. At any point it has various product messages to get across, and a number of emotional or self-image benefits. They have used a longitudinal model. For any given execution the Creative Strategy calls for a focused combination of product and self-image. But over time these combinations change, so that the full Levi's story is told—all held together by the Levi's "voice and attitude." Some of the car companies use this approach. I have even seen it on Tide, which for short periods diverges from its cleaning message to promote features like fabric care.[21]

Note, however, that in all these activities, individual executions are still focused.

QUESTION 4—ARE WE GETTING THERE?

As the effort goes to market, we must ask this. It involves the "hard" measures of shipments, share and profit. It will also often include diagnostic research into what the campaign has achieved, and why. The science here is to examine the trajectory of a brand before the new campaign, and decide what mile-markers will identify the changes. They could be attitude and awareness, and other variables in tracking. Or they could be more anecdotal, such as evidence from sales people and the media, or a change in a competitor's strategy.

---

20 The evidence is in every image study. Those ratings for benefits that the brands never talk about have to come from somewhere.

21 At one time, P&G would never have done this.

There's a point of best-practice here as well. Whatever tools you choose, define them before the campaign breaks, so that they are clearly understood in the heat of battle. Also, make the yardsticks flexible enough that you can still pick up unexpected signals with brand-building value.[22]

You then loop back to the first question, "Where are we now, and why," and your interrogation of the brand continues as a perpetual process.

The Role of the Strategist in Canada

I'd like to close by talking for a moment about how being a strategist in Canada differs from the experience in other countries. Six things drive the differences:

- The budgets we work with are smaller in absolute terms than for just about any other G8 nation (because of a nutty little thing called a small population).
- We must cover more geography and greater cultural differences without the ability to tailor messages (usually because of fact one).
- Therefore, we have the additional challenge of finding insights that are specifically *and* universally relevant.
- Our clients sometimes feel more comfortable with "global" research tools, when it might be more relevant to have made-in-Canada research tools.
- For more and more brands the really big-picture decisions are being made in another country.
- But, thanks to Canadian companies being smaller, we have a greater chance of lining up all of a brand's soldiers to support the strategy we create.

---

22 A striking example is the Cassies Grand Prix for the 1996 launch of the Chrysler NS Minivan. At launch, the driver's-side sliding door was not even standard, and it was one of four features being pushed. But early results showed that the new door was a huge hit. The entire launch plan was changed in mid-stream to focus exclusively on the door. The rest, as they say, is history, with over $500 million in incremental sales during the launch year.

This is a living breathing example of necessity being the mother of invention—not only in the solutions we come up with, but in *how* we come up with them.

I can't think of a better place to do what we do. Strategy is about making choices, and our environment forces us to do this better and smarter. What we lack in means we also make up for in access—to the sales force, to the trade, to top management, to our competitors, and to the media. That, it seems to me, creates greater opportunities for innovation.

All we maybe sometimes lack, other than big brand budgets, is the courage of our convictions. We are the world's second biggest consumers of insurance, after all.

Overview: Chapter Four

As Arthur Fleischmann says at the end of his chapter, briefing is "one of the most critical (but often most neglected) aspects of the creative development process." He's right.

There's something about us humans that makes effective communication elusive. Arthur refers to the game of broken telephone. It's an example of what we might call Murphy's Law of Communication:

Anything that can be misunderstood will be misunderstood.

I've known a few people who find briefing, especially creative briefing, difficult or even tiresome. If any readers are in this camp, I hope this chapter changes your minds. A great brief is not a dashed-off version of you-know-what-I-mean. There is a rare skill to doing it well, but the results make it very much worth the effort.

The chapter makes an important distinction between "The Brief" and "Brief-ING." The first is the formal document that most systems require, and the second is all the activity that surrounds it.

There are different, and sometimes controversial philosophies about briefing too. The chapter covers these in some detail, before closing with a review of the approach at john st.

Chapter Four

Briefing—Increasing the Odds of Success

ARTHUR FLEISCHMANN

Introduction

In another place and time, Lewis Carroll might have gone into advertising. His alter-ego, the Cheshire Cat, certainly grasped the critical importance of a clear brief.

> "Would you tell me please which way I ought to go from here?" asked Alice.
> "That depends a good deal on where you want to go to," said the Cat.
> "I don't much care where," said Alice.
> "Then it doesn't matter which way you go," said the Cat.

While clients and agencies may lament the state of their advertising, perhaps a good place to start is by examining how they got there in the first place. In briefing, there are many ways to get to the destination, and all the different processes have their special points. The way you go will depend a lot on the advertising philosophy at the client and the agency. But *how* you go—the mood, motivation and atmosphere—will depend a lot on you. Over the years, I've worked with most of the main approaches, so I thought it would be helpful to paint a picture of the broader landscape. We also have our own approach at john st., and I'll also talk about that. As readers, you can then pick and choose the ideas that work best in your situation.

This brings me to the title.

I once saw a study that said, on average, people remember just one ad[1] from the previous evening in front of the TV. How can you increase the odds it will be for your brand? Without a concise, credible and inspiring brief, you're likely doomed from the start.

> *The greatest challenge is to create a brief with a compelling, simple idea.*
>
> *And the best ideas are rooted in a truth that unites the consumer, the category, and the brand.*

Let's look at what has been learned about making this happen.

The Target Audience for This Chapter

All good briefings take a lot of care defining the target audience, and I'm going to do the same. In the broadest sense, there is a role for all of the following:

- The client marketing team (at all levels).
- The agency account management, planning, and creative people.
- Media people.
- Direct Response, Interactive, Sales Promotion, Event Marketing, PR, and so on.

However, for focus, I am going to single out the client/account management/planning/creative team. As we will see, there are different ideas about how these four disciplines should interact.

Why All the Fuss?

I've known people on the client side who've said "what's the big deal over briefing? The agency knows what we want—to make our brand

---

1   In the appropriate brand-linked way, of course.

as strong and profitable as possible, short *and* long term. The brand benefits are pretty clear. Why can't they just get on with it?"

They have a point, if they are lucky enough to have a brand with an exciting and relevant point of difference (to consumers, not just the internal team). However, most of us live in a world that Alvin Toffler called over-choiced.[2] With over 20,000 SKUs in the supermarket, more than 1,000 mutual funds (poorly performing, as I write this chapter), and dozens of cellular communications options, how can we expect consumers to embrace and stay loyal to our brand? By having a simple, compelling proposition that intrigues them.

More often than not, this is expressed in some form of advertising. So if we all do our jobs well, advertising can become a brand's greatest competitive advantage. A powerful, simple idea expressed through compelling advertising will set the stage for an entire *brand culture.* Some of the examples we explore later demonstrate how simple ideas, created at the briefing stage, mushroomed into long-term advertising campaigns—and even more interestingly—defined how the client managed all aspects of the brand.

But this can only happen if the entire team is on board. This is why active, visible, senior involvement from the client is essential.

The Essence of a Great Brief

A great brief comes down to four things, and they are all important:

- It sets a clear direction.
- It inspires the creative team
- It springs from a deep and powerful insight.
- It sets the parameters by which the advertising will be assessed.

a) *Clear Direction*

What goes into a brief makes an immense difference to what comes out. My colleague in the UK version of this book uses the analogy of the supertanker. If the rudder is off by even a fraction the tanker finishes up miles off course.

---

2 From *Future Shock.*

b) Inspires the Creative Team

If I were hiring a lawyer or an accountant, and they told me that I had to "inspire my legal or accounting team," I would tell them where to get off. When it comes to creative, I've seen some clients (especially those who have never worked in an agency) react this way. But every act of creation requires inspiration—whether it's a book, a painting or an advertising idea. A creative team is more motivated when they see the creative potential. This will always be on the mind of the account group and planners, but clients have an immense effect here too, possibly more than the others because they have the ultimate decision-making power.

c) Insight

If you find the insight on the side of the pack, it probably isn't one. Consumers have been so bombarded with advertising messages that we must find *deeper ways* to connect with head and heart. If you're confused about insight versus superficial observation, think of standup comics. Jerry Seinfeld built a career picking up subtle points about people and situations. These truths resonate, and this is how insights do their magic.[3]

d) Parameters for Assessment

Advertising is a tool to do a job, and the job should be precisely defined. The advertising should then be assessed against what it has been asked to do.

In a nutshell, then, if you think about what a brief has to achieve:

> *A brief is an ad for the ad.*

---

3 Once in a while there's no great insight. The job then is to find the brilliantly effective creative solution anyway. See Jon Steel's *Truth, Lies & Advertising*.

The Nature Of Client Involvement

There are different views about the how the client and agency should interact for the best end result. They are on the following spectrum:

a) *The Scott Bedbury View*

This is at one extreme, as explained in *A New Brand World*:

> **The Value of Loose Briefs**
> One of the barriers preventing organizations from reaching their highest creative potential ... is the way in which the creative staff ... are briefed. Often, the briefs are too tight, mired with executional details and the like. In effect, they can become tourniquets. A great creative brief has three attributes. It is:
>
> 1. *Concise*—No more than two pages, one if you're really good.
> 2. *Tight*—Containing two separate focused statements: where the business (or category) and the brand are today, and where they must be tomorrow in order to achieve success.
> 3. *Loose*—Let them figure out how to get there.[4]

The packaged goods advertisers would find this horrifyingly open-ended, but Bedbury does have some modest brand-building success—at Nike and Starbucks—to support his point of view. It's also consistent with his attitude to creative. He relishes the unexpected, and for that reason does not demand the control built into some other approaches.

b) *Jon Steel's View*

Jon Steel is head of planning at Goodby, Silverstein & Partners—an agency with a track record of award-winning, business-building advertising. *Adweek* asked him to share his experience and he wrote *Truth, Lies & Advertising*. He is generally in line with Bedbury:

---

4 Andy Macaulay's chapter has the Bedbury brief that led to "Just Do It."

Clients should not participate in creative briefing. A brief is between, usually, a planner and account person on the one hand, and a creative team of art director and copywriter on the other. For this to work most effectively, it is important that clients take a back seat. I realize that many people, clients especially, may raise their eyebrows at this idea. Exclude the clients from the creative briefing? Surely that's heresy?

First, let me clarify what I mean by suggesting that clients not play a direct role, because it is not as subversive as it may sound. I think that they should always contribute to the thinking that provides the brief's foundation and should be in full agreement with the campaign objectives, proposed target, and the broad idea the creative team will be asked to communicate. Beyond that, however, they do not need to participate in the verbal briefing of the creative team and should not need to see a written brief at all. As long as they have agreed the general direction, then the detail should not concern them.[5]

c) Historical Practice

The mid-spectrum is dominated by thinking that originated in the packaged goods firms. As their alumnae have gone forth and multiplied, so have their systems:

- The client has a comprehensive view on how to brief the agency—often codified by head office.
- There is a formal process, with formats designed to stimulate, guide and capture the client/agency thinking.[6]
- Clients used to have the mindset, "this is what the agency needs to understand and embrace." More recently, the approach has become more collaborative (see next section), but it is still highly definitive.

---

5   His point is that many clients, however well meaning, give off a parental aura that inhibits the creative process. This is difficult to tell a client, but it is not at all uncommon.

6   There are two red flags here: (a) a tendency to "fill in the boxes," rather than wrestle with the deeper issues, (b) a tendency for senior clients to give the thinking that we might call a "sounds right to me" level of attention—only discovering after creative is presented that they do not agree with the brief. Guard against this.

- Clients accept that agencies will want to translate the client brief into an "agency brief."
- However, clients sometimes felt that the reinterpretation was off the mark. So many now insist that they sign off on the agency's internal brief.[7]
- The end result is, ideally, a rigorous and imaginative piece of thinking, understood and embraced at all levels of client and agency, laying out a clear and inspiring direction for brand success.

This approach has worked well enough, though my personal view is that its effectiveness (or lack of it) relates more to the people than the process itself.

d) Current Evolution

Some clients and agencies are developing approaches that bring the client and agency together more. This often starts with an upfront event. The idea is to create a hothouse effect, with key players from all sides getting together to define (and hopefully start to crack) the issue at hand. These events are a mix of blue sky and discipline, and take a great deal of skill and talent to pull off well. Many agencies have a proprietary name for their approach. Clients are intimately involved.

e) Where to Be on the Spectrum?

Across the myriad client/agency partnerships, there are multiple variations of all this. As we'll see, john st. happens to be at the collaborative end of the spectrum.[8] But my purpose isn't to persuade you to one approach or another. That choice will depend on the beliefs and culture of the client and the agency. All of these approaches are effective when done well. All go off the rails when done badly.

---

7 Bedbury and Steel are not in this camp, but many are. It ensures that everyone is on board, and helps avoid the problems in the preceding footnote.

8 Bedbury and Steel endorse a collaborative *attitude*—but they feel that the advertising will usually be better if the agency is left largely on its own after the direction is set.

Some Loose Ends

Before we get down to specific tips, there are some things to tidy up.

a) Strategy versus Briefing

Some people see "creative strategy" and "creative briefing" as different, and are meticulous in maintaining a distinction. Others use the terms interchangeably. And "strategy" gets used with countless different meanings anyway. Rather than try to thread this needle, I'll just ask readers to substitute the terminology that works for them.

b) Brief versus Brief-ING

A project starts with a business goal at one end, and a creative solution at the other. The Brief is the main piece of thinking that bridges the gap. It is encapsulated in a document, and discussed at the Briefing Meeting. It defines the task at hand.

Brief-ING, on the other hand, is continuous. The client role will depend on the spectrum discussed earlier, but for account people and planners it is an intuitive dance with the creative team—seeding ideas, answering questions, base-touching, handholding, or just staying out of the way—always with an eye to getting the best solution. Brief-ING is the lubricant that helps get the best out of the process.

c) The Strategic versus the Tactical Brief

All the great brands have a distinct sense of what makes them what they are. Even in this happy position, the brief for new activity will still need careful thought (it can be lethal to rest on one's laurels), but it may well be right to be tactical—i.e. to refresh what is working, while staying "true to the brand."[9] A bigger challenge is when you need a new brand-defining campaign. There will be tussles about the degree of change—with some wanting to retain the current effort, and others pushing for a complete overhaul.

---

9 This is not as easy as it sounds, because you can't "refresh" without change, and there can be heated debates about the degree of change that is indeed "true to the brand." See "Staying the Course while Staying Fresh" in the Appendix to Chapter 1.

Either way, the brand needs a Strategic Brief. Some systems make a distinction between this type of document and the tactical one. But whatever the paperwork, make sure the task has been thought through and clearly defined.

d) Media Neutrality

There was a time when it was pretty much assumed by clients and agencies that major brand-building activity (in terms of communication) would centre on advertising. Many of the great brands came out of this era.

We now think in terms of "every point of contact," and assess the role of all the different media—advertising being just one. However, this new model still needs a "core idea" to define the brand. I embrace the view that it can originate in any of the disciplines,[10] but for this chapter will assume that it is most likely to spring from the client/account management/planning/creative foursome.

e) Formats

Most people have client or agency formats. They cover similar territory, although the terminology can reveal different philosophies about how advertising and brand-building work. Jon Steel has an aversion to formats—because in his view they encourage shallow thinking (or its anal-compulsive companion: haggling over words to the detriment of insights and ideas). He asks a brief to answer seven questions, in plain English, as insightfully[11] as possible:

- Why are we advertising at all?
- What is the advertising trying to achieve?
- Who are we talking to?
- What do we know about them?
- What's the main idea we need to communicate?
- What's the best way of planting that idea?
- How do we know we're right? (This is an internal explanation—not something that goes in the advertising.)

---

10 Alan Middleton talks to this point in his chapter on IMC.
11 And, based on the examples in *Truth, Lies & Advertising*, at some length.

Note that there is no Support or Reason Why. Steel (originally out of the UK) does not advocate "Benefit/Reason Why" thinking, which largely originated in the US.

Today, as products have become commodities, Steel's thinking makes sense. Unless you have some truly exciting and unique benefit, your brand's success will rely often on your ability to create an emotional bond—a much tougher task.

Steel's view is that benefits and reasons why play a role, but that the brief should focus on what people *should take away from the advertising,* rather than on what the advertiser should put in. In other words, the "main idea" does not specify what the advertising should say, but the response it will get.

f) A Message to the Creative People

If you complain about briefings—which would perpetuate a long-standing tradition—do something about it. A great brief has had an insight or idea that no one has had before. This is one of your strengths. So take an active role. The days of "waiting for the brief" are long gone.[12]

Creating a Great Brief

This is about the brief as a document. Most of the tips apply to clients as well as the agency, though this will vary with the degree of client involvement:

a) The Role of Advertising

The goal is to inspire the creative team, so capture this *simply.* Is it really helpful to put "advertising must increase awareness leading to trial of brand X"? Every aspect of the brief must evoke, provoke and inspire. Try stage-setting like this:

---

12 Ian Mirlin makes the same point in his chapter.

- Make Labatt Blue appeal to a new generation of beer drinkers.
- Make Sunlight the brand of choice to those who switch between Tide and Sunlight.
- Make Clarica the insurance brand that stands for clarity.

Some approaches call for numerical objectives—for ad awareness, message communication and so forth. These can be important from the business point of view, but most creative teams are number-phobic. If this section includes numbers, keep them separate.

b) Be Realistic about What Can Be Achieved for the Budget.

As a client, there is often less to invest than you might want for your brand. But don't play the "challenge" game—where you exhort the agency to deliver silk purse results with a sow's ear budget.

There could hardly be a worse idea for increasing the odds of success. The agency is in a cleft stick. It either has to accept an unrealistic challenge, or tell you that your goals are out of kilter. Either way, motivation drops like a stone. Far better is to use your combined knowledge to arrive at a realistic plan.[13]

c) Be Utterly Focused.

Many people agree, but then create a maze of objectives. For understandable reasons, clients are prone to this, and we in advertising have to do a better job convincing them that effectiveness comes from simplicity.[14]

Incidentally, the solution is not to string things together—you know the idea: *an unsurpassed combination of taste and nutrition in a handy, fun-filled pack.*

---

13 This would be easier if there were hard and fast rules, but it takes a combination of judgment and experience. Case histories such as the Cassies can be useful.

14 See related comments in Andy Macaulay's chapter on Strategy.

d) Define the Target as an Audience of One.

Marketing people and creative people don't look at target audiences the same way, and this has to be reconciled in the brief. There are two aspects to this:

- Defining and describing the Primary Audience.
- Handling Secondary or even Tertiary Audiences.

From a marketing point of view, the audience has to be big enough to support the brand. For example, something as broad as women 18–49. But there are enormous differences in these women. Creative people work best if they live and breathe the life of the target, so bring one person to life. And don't worry about who you are missing out. Advertising created for the "audience of one" still has power against the broader audience—it's like a bell curve. And it's far more effective than a bland effort that tries to appeal to everyone.

There are a number of ways to picture the audience of one. Try mapping out a day in the life of the target. Follow your target around for a few days. Get them on film. Use syndicated studies to understand their attitudes toward different topics. Bring them to life as real people, warts and all.

As to Secondary and Tertiary Audiences, be hard-nosed about whether they should be included at all. Here again there are two questions to answer:

- Do you need different messages for different audiences?
- Do you try to create one approach that works for all?

If you are in this situation, and write "appealing to x, while not alienating y" be careful. This is not necessarily wrong, but there is a big risk that you will dilute the end product. Even an objective like "appealing to Moms while also appealing to kids" sounds plausible until you try to create the advertising. As a team, think through what the risks really are. In my experience they are less than we typically worry about. The far bigger risk is not being noticed.

e) Find the Compelling, Simple Thought.

This is the heart of the brief. It makes it inescapably clear what the creative team has to work to. If as account person or planner you aren't coming up with anything insightful, get the creative team involved. This part of the brief is sometimes called the Key Consumer Benefit, or the Proposition etc. There was a time when it could be quite straightforward, but nowadays that only gets you to first base. Here's a comment from Angus Tucker, one of my partners, and co-creative director at john st.

> Getting to a great brief takes one thing—distillation. One thought. When the creative team asks, "what am I trying to say here?" the planner or account person has to be able to answer in one sentence. And that answer should immediately start sparking ideas. The brief for Sunlight could have said, "Sunlight gets clothes their cleanest" but as Truman Capote would say, that's not writing, that's typing. The thought "Sunlight is an invitation to get dirty" is the best brief I've ever heard of.

Here are some examples of straightforward and imaginative propositions. Notice how the imaginative ones have dug deeper in their search for a truth that links the consumer, the category, and the brand:

- (Straightforward) Milk is refreshingly good for you.
- (Imaginative) Milk: Imagine your life without it.[15]
- (Straightforward) Fujifilm helps you take beautiful photographs.
- (Imaginative) Fujifilm encourages people to look beyond the obvious.
- (Straightforward) Cuervo Tequila: Good Drinks. Fun Times. Real People.
- (Imaginative) Cuervo Tequila: A party waiting to happen.[16]

---

15 From the US "Got Milk" campaign, based on milk deprivation.

16 Jon Steel uses Cuervo to illustrate the dangers of a multiple benefit driven by research. Good Drinks, Fun Times, and Real People were the "winners" in a mapping exercise. As he points out, this utterly failed to uncover the essence of the brand.

f) Cut Out Anything That Will Cloud the Focus.

Some briefs are anything but brief. They may have multiple objectives. They may contain the information that justifies the decisions from a business point of view. They may have extensive data about the brand's history, competition, market trends, and so forth. All of this is important in deciding what to do, but it is not necessarily needed after that. Here's a guideline:

> Knowing the way the creative team works, include anything that may spark an idea. Leave the rest out, or put it in an Appendix.

g) Use "Reason Why" as a Stimulus, Not a Straightjacket.

This needs care. In some situations, the reason why has to be mandatory. Crest has been mentioned elsewhere in this book. Its advertising always had "contains fluoride" and "endorsed by the American or Canadian Dental Association." A Crest brief would be explicit, and say that these support points must appear.

In other situations, the reasons why are *optional*. They are an inventory of facts that *might* stimulate an idea, but the creative team doesn't have to use them if they don't have to. Eggs, in Andy Macaulay's chapter, would be an example. The team seized on the thought that eggs come in nature's own package. This type of support point should be put under a heading such as "this could be helpful."

The distinction—between mandatory and optional—bears repeating. Too much advertising is cluttered with points. They were often in the brief under the guise of being optional, but come approval time were treated as mandatory.

Separately, some brands have no obvious reason why. Energizer? Maytag? Volkswagen? Tide has rarely had a "magic ingredient." And then there's Nike. In other words, decide if you need a reason why at all, and only then of what type.[17]

---

17 Many people insist on a reason-why, but the success of these brands can't be ignored. The answer seems to be that if you stake out a benefit in a highly convincing way a reason-why can sometimes complicate, rather than enhance, the story.

h) Write for the Creative Team.

Creative people admire things that are well written. Write in clear everyday English, not gobbledygook.[18]

i) Offer Sandboxes—if the Creative Team Wants Them.

Sandboxes are areas to play in, all on strategy of course. Some creative teams like them. Some do not. Jon Steel advocates them in his book. Polaroid invented instant pictures, but over time they lost that uniqueness. They needed a new stance, and arrived at the following—with Polaroid, the picture is only the beginning. The planner suggested several ways (sandboxes) to bring this notion to life. Some are captured here:

> Maybe highlight the innovative or unusual ways that people are using Polaroid—at home and at work.
>
> Perhaps focus on the effects of a Polaroid picture ... the chain of events that sets it in motion.
>
> I took the picture *so* something would happen, *for* a certain reason, *to* achieve a particular objective.
>
> Think about how Polaroid pictures ... can be a language themselves.

Note that these are suggestions, not directives. Also that the creative solution was triggered by the sandboxes, but was not unique to any particular one. The "See What Develops" campaign shows Polaroid pictures capturing dramatic moments: a neighbour's dog fouling the lawn, a wife who puts a seductive picture in her husband's briefcase, and so on. [19]

j) Don't Work in Isolation.

No one advocates solitary toil in an attic. If you are the lead person on a brief you will need quiet time on your own, but do bring in others. The rough and tumble of debate leads to better answers in the end.

---

18 There used to be a belief that a brief should contain words alone, out of a fear that visuals and music create preconceptions. That fear has largely gone away.

19 This is why some creative teams hate sandboxes. They can create the expectation of a particular solution rather than—as in this case—stimulating a new one.

k) Be Thoughtful About Tone & Manner.

This articulates the delivery that will help the audience process the message, while being in-sync with the brand's long-term personality or character. Misuses can send you astray, so let's review the main problems:

- *Motherhood.* Words like "convincing" and "believable." They aren't wrong, but are so self-evident as to be worthless. (Try the opposites test. Can you imagine wanting to be unconvincing, or unbelievable?)

- *Clichés.* Words like "authoritative" and "fun" may not be wrong, but they will not electrify the creative team.

- *Oxymorons.* These are amazingly common, and can be picked out by the inclusion of "but", "yet," or "while." Concoctions like "aggressive and assertive, yet empathetic and understanding."

- *Divergent Combinations.* These can be valid on paper, but are devilishly hard to capture in actual tone and manner—for example, "As befits a dynamic leader, but with the common touch."

- *Counter-Intuitives.* For some brands logic will mislead you. Think about Raid. It's a high-performance killer. What tone and manner would seem right? Certainly not a cartoon campaign.[20]

l) Specify Brand Personality/Brand Character.

Tone & Manner describes the *advertising,* and some argue that it should depend on the task at hand. They regard Brand Personality or Character as much more important. It captures the brand (as it is, or as you want it to be) in human terms. In many cases Brand Personality/Character will be very close to Tone & Manner. But sometimes (as with Raid) it will be different. Duracell is an "authoritative leader," but its advertising, for years, showed cute little toys. American Express and IBM also fit this mould. They have a "significant and substantial" Brand Character, but their advertising often has a light touch. As with many of these debates, there is an argument on both sides, and you have to think the issues through.

---

20 The cartoon idea apparently came from creative intuition. People want bugs dead, but they absolutely don't want to be confronted with writhing, dying, real insects.

m) Be Sparing with Executional Considerations.

One of the surest ways to kill a brilliantly original solution is to burden it with preconceived requirements.

n) Love What You Do, but Don't Fall in Love with the Brief.

Planners do themselves and the process a disservice if they fall in love with their idea, particularly in the early stages. Be open-minded to various ways of cracking the problem. We all want to crack the problem quickly, but deciding too fast may shut down great ideas waiting to be discovered.

Brief-ING

This section is about the process that accompanies the Brief. The first two points refer to client briefing. The rest mainly refer to internal agency briefing.

a) Have the Top Client Decision-Maker at the Client Briefing.

Despite the issues at stake (to say nothing of the investment), senior clients often do not attend this meeting. But a briefing always triggers hopes, fears, flashes of ideas, blind alleys, sudden insights, miscues, questions—all the chaos of the creative melting pot. The senior decision-maker needs to be there.

b) For Client or Internal Briefings, Make the Meeting an Event.

Imagine smashing a hole in the wall, and then repairing it, to get everyone excited about a Polyfilla type product. Or decking out the room like a Parisian café for a brand with a European flair. Or laminating the brief for Speedo Swimwear, and dropping it in a swimming pool for the creative team to retrieve.

But be careful. Some teams love this sort of thing, but not all, especially if they think you are using showbiz to gussy up some average thinking. But in general, doing something imaginative to kick off the process works.

The main thing is relevance. One account person gave the creative team a cell phone and called them with instructions to meet up at various watering holes. The brief was for a beer promotion. Cases of beer were to be seeded with a cell phone or beeper, and the lucky winner would be invited to private parties and concerts. Another washed one side of his Bouvier Des Flanders with Pert Plus, the other side with "the leading shampoo." The dog may not have been pleased, but the creative team got the point. For anything but the most routine of projects, make the briefing meeting special. In particular, never send a briefing through the mail, or even worse, dash off something via e-mail. The stakes are too high.

c) Make the Brief Visual.

It's amazing how many briefings take place in a plain room, with a word-heavy document or a Powerpoint presentation. In his chapter, Ian Mirlin talks about the need for *visual stimulus.* At a minimum, have your product and competitive product in the room. Ditto for the advertising. Pictures of the target audience are also a great idea. Maybe add theatre by using/trying/demonstrating the product. Or the competitive product. Perhaps play the "day in the life" game. Perhaps play music. Whatever it is, get the meeting out of the words-only straightjacket.

d) Sprinkle with Factoids.

This applies to the client briefing, but is perhaps better done during the internal agency process—because you have to thread a path between overload and stimulation. The creative mind can seize on a fact that no one else noticed, and turn it into a brilliantly compelling idea.[21] But that same creative mind dozes when the information is boring from a creative point of view. Creative people can also get excited about red herrings. For all these reasons, there is an art to factoid sprinkling. Work to get the balance right.

---

21 Rupert Brendon cites British Airways. Ten million or so North Atlantic passengers is about as dull as it gets. "Manhattan Landing" is exhilarating.

e) Use the Heads-up if it Works for the Creative Team.

This is an internal point, but it's good for clients to be aware of it. Quite often, the strategy/brief process takes longer than planned, and creative development time gets squeezed. If the creative team is part of strategy development they can see this coming. But if they are not, do you give them a heads-up so that they can start thinking ahead of the approved brief?

Strictly speaking, you don't mobilize the team until a brief is approved, because it's not in anyone's interest to send creative people on a wild goose chase. But what if the team *wants* a heads-up? Give them information that can percolate into their subconscious. How do you know if they want it? Ask.

f) Don't Cry Wolf.

Deadlines, priorities, and procrastination are a constant source of pressure. A planner or account person (or client) may handle this in different ways, but *don't* create false deadlines. The team always find out, and your credibility is precious. Don't devalue it.

g) Develop the Art of Dropping By.

In Brief-ING there is a mating dance. Desmond Morris would recognize the rituals. Creative people know the steps on the client/ planning/ account management side, and the same is true the other way.

If you have ever experienced "the tyranny of the blank page" you know why creative people procrastinate. If you know how fragile ideas are, you understand why teams don't want to show you work in progress. And if, from the creative side, you have any clue what it feels like to wait and wonder, you understand why people need to know how you are doing.[22]

This is why we must give the creative team space, but also stay in touch. There is no checklist for this, except to say that constant hovering and constant silence are both wrong.

---

22 Compare it to waiting for a jury to come in with a verdict. They take as long as it takes. Meanwhile, your life is in the balance.

Some people have a knack for getting it right, and if you do that's wonderful. If you aren't sure, talk to the team and work out what's best. When the dynamic is good, most creative teams prefer short, spontaneous jam sessions with the planner or a key account person during creative development. It helps ensure their early thinking is on track, and gives them a sounding board.

h) Be Positive.

Briefing is about direction *and* motivation. Some people are so keen to keep the team on track that they move into a "don't" mode. Keep the mood stimulating and positive.

(I want to make a point here to clients. If you have not worked on the agency side you probably have no idea how much you affect motivation. Of course you have responsibility for direction and approvals, but this is not where motivation occurs. It's the environment you create, and the way you help ideas happen. I ask you to see yourselves as *catalyst*s.)

i) Be Helpful.

As the creative juices start flowing, the team often wants more information. This is a great sign. Once in a while it will be a drag to get it, but do it cheerfully—this is one of the ways you can be the catalyst to a great idea. Also, once the brief is complete, the planner/account thinking isn't done. Keep looking for ways to bring the idea to life. Sometimes an unusual media or promotional idea will spark a great campaign idea. Don't wait to be asked—take the initiative.

j) Do What's Right for the Brand.

This is your anchor. In any complicated situation, whatever the forces on you, make this the guiding principle.

This look at general principles should help you increase your odds of success. Rupert Brendon and David Rutherford also asked me to describe how we work at john st.

Briefing at john st.

In most creative development processes, the strategy, brief and creative are seen as distinct stages. All too often it becomes like the childhood game of broken telephone. First comes the translation of business strategy to marketing strategy; then marketing strategy to communication strategy; communication strategy to advertising strategy; advertising strategy to advertising brief; advertising brief to creative idea; and finally creative idea to executions.

At each stage we increase the chances of overcomplicating the advertising, overthinking the answers, and developing advertising that goes unnoticed. And the greatest risk in advertising isn't creating shocking or off-character advertising. It's creating advertising that, despite the millions spent in media, goes unnoticed.

So how do we connect the problem that advertising must solve to the creative idea? We unabashedly believe in blurring the line between creative and strategic development.

We bring the client, planning, creative and account team together from the start (the Ground Floor Session), all the way through the search and identification of key insights to the development of what we call the Brand Idea.

The Ground Floor Session

Most agencies have some sort of kickoff jam session, often centred on the client brief. A well-facilitated session, with insightful and imaginative questions and exercises, helps uncover the real challenge to be solved by advertising.

In our case, we work together to profile what role the category and brand play in our consumer's life. We often challenge the fundamentals the client holds dear: what business are they *really* in? Are breweries in the beer business or the fun business? Is Sunlight in the detergent business or the freedom business? Is Fujifilm in the photography business or the creativity business? For Clarica Insurance, oddly enough, the big "aha" came when we determined they weren't in the insurance business, but rather in the *clarity* business.

There are added benefits of this type of session. By having key decision-makers sequestered and focused on nothing but the communication challenge, we open dialogue between agency and client—with senior clients who seldom have the time to focus on their advertising. Furthermore, because creative teams are key participants, they start thinking about the problem and possible solutions early in the process.

Gathering Insights

All agencies cull research for a powerful fact or observation on which to base an advertising idea. The challenge is finding an insight that forms a logical story linking the category, the consumer, and the brand. We find that it helps to think of this graphically:

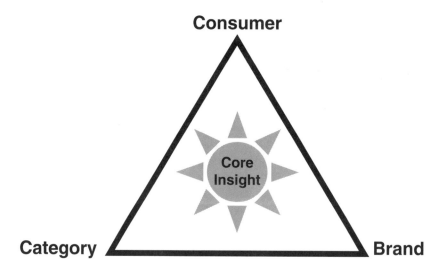

For connecting the category and the consumer we look for relevance—
the fit with lifestyle, behaviour and attitudes. For connecting the consumer to the brand we look for linkages the brand can own. And for
connecting the brand to the category we look for distinctiveness and
salience.

Bringing the three together allows us to tell a story about the
brand and its role in a person's life. In making these connections, we
look for insights beyond the obvious, and once we have distilled a
range of them, we share them as an agency and client team. In this
way we check our thinking and get early buy-in. On Sunlight, for
example:

Consumer

Sunlight/Tide switchers think doing laundry is a
drag. But having the freedom to get dirty is a
contemporary way of saying "clean."

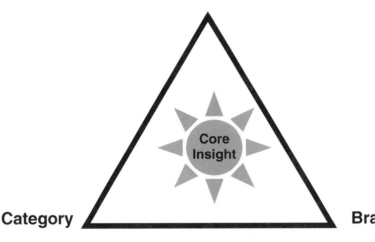

Category

Tide, the leading competitor, owns
the category benefit of "cleans
whiter than white."

Brand

Sunlight is a likable, inviting, more
youthful brand. However, it doesn't
have cleaning credentials.

On Clarica, our team developed this at our former agency, Ammirati Puris:

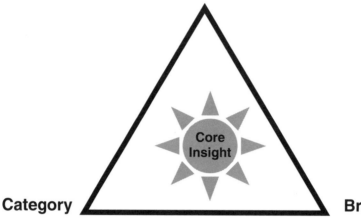

Consumer

In all walks of life, people seek a greater sense of simplicity, resulting in a greater sense of control and ultimately comfort.

Core Insight

Category

Clarity is most desired, yet most lacking, in the financial and insurance category, because companies needlessly confuse the average person.

Brand

Clarica agents and employees create clarity through plain-speak.

The Strategic Idea

Call it a strategic idea, a positioning, an essence, whatever (we call it a Brand Idea) the result has to be a concise, compelling and long-term proposition for the brand. Sunlight is an invitation to get dirty. Clarica: there's a lot to be said for clarity. A whole lot can happen out of the Blue. As a planner/creative/account team we work to turn these into consumer-friendly and inspiring expressions.

Refining the Brand Ideas

We hold work sessions with consumers, and the creative team is always there. This research puts more emphasis on creating than it does on "testing." For example, while we will often have four or five ideas going into these focus groups, the best idea can come from a fusion of them, or from something new that comes up.

Clarica. Washroom :30

1. Guy looks at abstract signs on washroom doors in a restaurant

2. He squints uncertainly.

3. The toilet flushes behind one of the doors.

4. A very androgynous person walks out.

5. He looks at him/her uncertainly.

6. Clarica. Investment and insurance solutions. Since 1870.

Since people think in pictures, why should ideas be only in words? We pair our strategic thoughts with visual stimuli. This helps us convey the idea internally and to consumers. And why stop there? For highly emotional categories, we might add music, a colour palette, and other aesthetic stimuli to convey the idea more evocatively. Here are some visuals that helped shape the idea that a whole lot can happen out of the Blue:

"The best times come from out of the Blue."

The Briefing

Because the briefing is a complete process that includes the client from the beginning, the internal (agency) briefing is often, in the best sense, anticlimactic. By this point we've defined what business the client is really in; we've tested and distilled a single Brand Idea; we've even created a visual and textual briefing tool—we call it the Brand Portrait—which distills the look, tone & manner, emotional, and (if any) rational promise of the brand. Our Cassies-winning campaign on Lipton came from such a process.

Lipton Chicken Noodle Soup: Whoopie Cushion :30

1. Dad walks into living room and sits down.

2. SFX: Whoopie Cushion.

3. Mom walks into kitchen and sits down.

4. SFX: Whoopie Cushion.

5. Sis sits on cushion. SUPER: kid's don't get bored of what they like.

6. SUPER: They like Lipton Chicken Noodle Soup.

The creative team, planners, account managers, and client have been involved from the beginning, so what's left? We hold another jam session that's somewhere between a brief and a brainstorm. Here we look for different ways to put the Brand Idea in front of the consumer. In doing so, we generate a number of tactical ideas but more importantly, we spark campaign and executional ideas. Like any jam session, this one must be adeptly facilitated to ensure the right areas are explored and the best ideas are brought forward.

After all this, the briefing document can be a non-event. It is often like a contact report, rather than a breakthrough document featuring new thinking. The remainder of the process involves small and often spontaneous discussions between creative and planners. As mentioned earlier, this gives creative teams a sounding board for early ideas, and planners or account people the opportunity to share new stimuli and ideas.

Summary: A Surprising Foregone Conclusion

This whole process is designed to be seamless and dynamic. The client and agency have dialogue and work sessions through every phase of discovery and development. Meanwhile, the numerous check points reduce disappointments, false starts and do-overs. No system is perfect, but when we present final creative concepts to the client, this one frequently has a beautiful end result—something that we call a surprising foregone conclusion.

I encourage you to experiment with different approaches. Once you find techniques that work, institutionalize them. You'll be a hero for helping facilitate and improve one of the most critical (but often most neglected) aspects of the creative development process.

Bibliography

Bedbury, S. (2002). *A New Brand World: 8 Principles for Achieving Brand Leadership in the 21st Century.* New York: Viking.
Cooper, A. ed. (1997). *How to Plan Advertising.* London: Cassell.
Steel, J. (1998). *Truth, Lies & Advertising: The Art of Account Planning.* New York: Wiley.
Toffler, A. (1970). *Future Shock.* London: Pan Books
www.cassies.ca for Sunlight and Clarica, plus other case histories.

Overview: Chapter Five

Most of this book is written to senior people. So is this chapter, but it has an ingenious way in.

Ian Mirlin has constructed it as advice to junior creative people. However, his real audience is the senior echelon—at the client and the agency. Ian points out that despite all the talk of change, we are missing a critical opportunity—to redefine the role of "the creative mind."

Ian is a copywriter by trade, and is regarded as one of Canada's finest. He is also the Mirlin of Harrod & Mirlin, and more recently has become the Chief Creative Officer at Young & Rubicam. As President at Harrod & Mirlin, he guided the agency through several incarnations—from local independent to part of a full-fledged multinational network.

This background has given him a view of the inner sanctum of business that many creative folk never see, and is the driving force behind his view of where the partnership of client and agency should be going.

There are no diagrams or checklists, just an exploration of ideas from a man who has seen this business from many different angles. Enjoy the journey.

Chapter Five

The Creative Responsibility

IAN MIRLIN

Introduction

If you were starting out as a copywriter or art director during the creative renaissance of the mid-60s, the chapter you are about to read would have begun with far simpler counsel: Shut your office door. Drink coffee. Have a cigarette. Do whatever it takes, just be brilliant.

Your responsibilities would have been radically different to what they are today. Most significantly: Bill Bernbach, the great godfather of the creative revolution that began in his agency, would have blanched at the thought of bringing creative people into too close proximity with the client.

The Doyle Dane Bernbach of the 60s believed that distance did indeed lend enchantment to the view, and that the creative mind was meant to float free of the hurly-burly of the client's business and its sales force/merchandizing/distribution/ production capacity issues, in order to find the groundbreaking creative solution. It was a time in which these aspects of the client's business were left to the agency's account people.

One can appreciate how Bernbach came to his point of view. It has long been held that great creative leaps are gained intuitively, more through feel than through logic, and that by overexposing the sensitive antennae of the creative mind to harsh realities, any breakthrough idea can be compromised before it has had time to draw its first breath.

Looking back at it now, DDB's legendary Volkswagen campaign is interesting in how it manifests the agency's creative philosophy. Legitimately seen as one of the great advertising campaigns of all time, the

Lemon.

This Volkswagen missed the boat.

The chrome strip on the glove compartment is blemished and must be replaced. Chances are you wouldn't have noticed it; Inspector Kurt Kröner did.

There are 3,389 men at our Wolfsburg factory with only one job: to inspect Volkswagens at each stage of production. (3000 Volkswagens are produced daily; there are more inspectors than cars.)

Every shock absorber is tested (spot checking won't do), every windshield is scanned. VWs have been rejected for surface scratches barely visible to the eye.

Final inspection is really something! VW inspectors run each car off the line onto the Funktionsprüfstand (car test stand), tote up 189 check points, gun ahead to the automatic brake stand, and say "no" to one VW out of fifty.

This preoccupation with detail means the VW lasts longer and requires less maintenance, by and large, than other cars. (It also means a used VW depreciates less than any other car.)

We pluck the lemons; you get the plums.

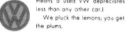

product, one may say, is treated with a sense of veneration produced by the sheltered distance of the creative team.

The "bug" photographed against its pristine white background is somewhat objectified. Admired from afar, as it were. While Helmut Krone's classic design was very much the product of an agency rewriting the rules of creativity in advertising, beneath this one might find clues to a particular period and what it asked of a creative person's role in an ad agency.

Today, that role has been drastically rewritten. Like most other businesses, advertising is under far greater pressure to deliver, is far more measured and monitored for its ability to affect sales. As a result, clients are demanding more direct involvement with the people responsible for doing the work. And although that takes into account everybody associated with the business, it is the agency's creative people who are most on the front line.

Despite their need for this greater accessibility, not all clients are driven by the same goal. Some want the creative input in order to factor a slightly more lateral, intuitive viewpoint into their own decision-making. Others are driving towards what they perceive as a more effective model for the agency/client relationship, in which the perceived "middle-people" play less of a role, and the client and those responsible for making the advertising enjoy unfettered access to one another. Yet another group see creative as the ultimate product the agency delivers and want an everyday contact, even a working intimacy, with those responsible for the work.

Whichever disposition might best describe the modern client, there is a new sandbox in which creative people have found themselves over the last decade. And it's a sandbox that very definitely asks our copywriters and art directors to open their vistas beyond copy and layout and accept a greater, more involved role.

Curiously, this shift in relationship and responsibility has not been given the discussion it deserves. Perhaps born out of the need to convince clients they were well prepared for the new paradigm, the agency process seemed to change silently in the middle of the night, and in the morning a new set of rules governed the creative mandate. Art directors and copywriters were suddenly learning new protocols. Some were simply learning how to dress more moderately.

While some opened their own agencies on the back of the revolution and proceeded to do good work, not enough was spoken about the new game or its rules. Future great talents germinating in our colleges of art, in our copy schools, or slaving over their portfolios in their bedrooms, were training for an olympics whose medal system had not been well explained. And what had to be explained was simply that the art of advertising had become the *business* of advertising, particularly for those responsible for the creative product. This seismic shift, with all its implications for our art directors and writers, had produced a brand new creative reality. And with it, an entirely redefined creative responsibility.

This is the new arena you will find yourself in. A place where you'll need to dazzle on a playing field that has been profoundly enlarged. To do great work, you can no longer simply assume responsibility for the creative product you generate within your personal office. Your sphere of influence must now include the strategic thinking, your clients' businesses and your relationships with your clients. Truth is, the creative responsibility is no longer simply the creative product but the entire process of making advertising.

Some will say it is the creative person's ability to impact the larger context that will determine the future of our industry and is becoming, more and more, the only path to doing great work that sells. Others may express an even more radical point of view—that the only way this business might remain creative is for the creative mind to influence every aspect of its workings.

"Creativity" said Arthur Koestler, "is the defeat of habit, by originality." While Koestler speaks to the creative imperative of always pursuing fresh, surprising work, his words provide an ironic comment for creative people in advertising. Unlike the independent artist free to roam the world in search of new creative inspiration and in so doing "break habit," the creative soul that finds itself in advertising is tied to a place and a protocol that inhibits true exploration simply by virtue of its repetitiveness: the research, the brief, the client's input, more research, etc.

The point here is that advertising paradoxically inhibits creative thinking because it's made through habitual process. That said, whatever else might change in the business, the process can't. It's the only viable pipeline we have. As endemic as the assembly line is to the manufacture of automobiles. Thus it is that the creative mind working in advertising has always been harnessed in some way, forced by the only practical model that exists to deliver habit-defeating ideas within a habitual environment.

Despite the fact that advertising agencies and their clients live in separate places, advertising has never been made on a separate agency-run assembly line. The micro context would reveal that its manufacture is actually *a part* of the client's assembly line. (A glance at any client's operating budget will show that the cost of the advertising is built into the operating costs.) This suffocating proximity makes the new challenge even more complex. The configurations of the business can't change. Bottom line is: we have to.

Speaking Two Languages

With the "you make the bagels, we'll make the ads" mentality a thing of the past, the creative mind today has to be oriented to first confront a client's business issues in the hope of then understanding the *role* that communication may play in solving that issue. (*Communication* being the operative word here—not *advertising*, as agencies adopt a less ad-centric, more media-neutral philosophy.)

Business and creativity however operate in two different languages. Peter Kim, a very fine planner at McCann's New York office, defined the difference between creativity and strategy most eloquently when he said:

> Strategy is the pursuit of passion through discipline. Creativity is the pursuit of discipline through passion.

If we read "strategy" as the language of business, we begin to understand the mindset and language necessary to this new enlarged creative role we described earlier, and the suppleness it demands for the creative person to be a broker of each. You will learn this bilingual sensibility simply through orientation and practice, but a good place to start is by attempting to fully understand the client's business in its most quintessential nature. By this I mean stripping back the apparent nature of that business and its superficial sales message, to discover the underlying *human truth* it appeals to. The value of this approach is that it tends to unearth, to the sophisticated client, his/her most sacred asset—making it instantly fertile ground upon which to establish common purpose. It also provides the richest area to explore for the creative solution. (I am one who believes all great communication, including advertising, fulfills its first responsibility when it reveals an aspect of humanity. Great advertising, when viewed by the appropriate customer, should generate the conscious or unconscious response: *"How did you know that about me?"*)

This stripping back is basically an exercise in reduction, ultimately providing a common lens that allows everyone involved to see the business the same way, from whatever discipline or vantage point they are viewing it, whether on the agency side or within the ranks of the client's operation.

While it is not within the parameters of this chapter to deal fully with this process of discovery, one can foresee from what's described above that the implications of an enlarged creative responsibility are far greater than one might have seen in years earlier. Creative truth can help provoke business truth, and a powerful business truth, when placed in sensitive client hands, can become an operational imperative.

The idea of the creative solution ultimately impacting the day-to-day operation of the client's business is by no means far-fetched and, in fact, is happening more and more frequently.

The buzzword that drove business in the 90s was integration. By that we meant a way of making sure all communications, individualized direct response, mainstream broadcast, promotion, and so on, spoke the same brand truth. Today, the word has a wiser, more sophisticated context. It denotes the unconditional union that must exist between a corporation's mission statement, its day-to-day operational values, and its outward brand promise.

Don't be surprised if the result of your thoroughness in exploring the brand for its "truth" is a path that leads naturally to this larger, more dramatic place where the external brand promise reflects your client's everyday internal reality. Nike Shoe Company in Beaverton, Oregon is a good example of how the creative responsibility at Wieden, Kennedy (their agency), and the business purpose of the organization itself, have merged to form an uncompromising, single-minded approach that guides everything they undertake.

Nike's brand mantra, *Authentic athletic performance,* and their mission statement, *To bring inspiration and innovation to every athlete in the world,* are dramatically illustrated in the agency's superb work and in Nike's corporate commitment to sponsoring some of professional sports' best (and most expensive) athletes. Nike's commitment includes even their underwriting the development of the USA's World Cup soccer team.

It is worth noting from the mission statement that it is *not* the company's apparent business (footwear) that forms its business focus, but rather the competitive spirit of the athlete. It makes a fascinating twist of strategy that Nike isn't interested in the feet of their customers, but rather in their minds.

It is through a clear sense of the brand's opportunity and (I would guess) a process of reduction similar to the one described earlier, that Nike has been able to arrive at that bedrock upon which they have fashioned their own proprietary human truth. I have always had a great deal of admiration for this client and their excellent agency for having used branding in so evolved and profound a way.

That advertising and brand communication in general can reach this level of elegance and effectiveness speaks to the role not only of the creative people involved on so significant a brand journey, but promotes a new grace and meaning to our craft that rescues it from its all too many detractors.

Insist on Access to the Key Decision-Makers

There are, as we know, many layers and trials through which good work has to pass in order for it to survive and still be brilliant. After the difficult birthing process, the work must pass an obstacle course of scrutiny within the agency, gain the necessary approvals from the client, and ultimately withstand the inevitable contribution of research— all of which conspires to make *less* of what was once probably *more*. It is a daunting journey indeed without having friends in high places to help provide safe passage for your work.

Fact is, there's simply no way for advertising to be truly meaningful without it being demanded and championed from the very top of the client's organization. This is very true of Nike and is most pertinent to their success. It's an unfortunate truth, but it is essentially impossible to do work of any consequence for a client whose culture and infrastructure do not demand and support it.

Assuming such a climate exists within the walls of the client's organization, it becomes vital that the creative team enjoys direct access to those who make the key decisions. Preferably the President him/herself. Now this of course supposes that the President has good advertising sensibilities, or that if he or she doesn't, there is a trusted someone who does. Seek out these key decision-makers. Talk to them about their company and their brands. Press them for the kind of information you intuitively feel will make for interesting work. Pursue that human truth.

A client once told me that the secret to getting useful, salient information from company presidents is not to ask them a long list of penetrating questions, but rather what they consider to be the recipe for success in their business.

From the answer, one can decipher all manner of implications such as their personal agenda, their business sensibilities, their (subjective) notion of what success actually means, etc. Importantly, you will gain an idea of what your role as a creative mind might be, working on their business.

Building relationships at this high level will help immeasurably in helping you understand the essential business objectives directly from the top, circumventing the dilution and unintended corruption that takes place through handed down information, allowing you to hear the subtleties that may spark imaginative answers.

The point here is simply: *You will not play at a higher level without access to higher places.* All superlative creative has had its champion, one may sometimes say its chief catalyst, propel the work from the corner office. Phil Knight is such a leader at Nike, as is Steve Jobs at Apple. Now of course there is a price to be paid for working in this rarefied atmosphere. It's the fact that you will need to lower the walls that previously gave you refuge while you nurtured your creative ideas, to now allow the client, in some way, to work alongside you.

This is difficult for many creative people to do. To be honest, I have personally found it challenging to deal with too much client closeness at times, the kind particularly that leads to commentary on "work in progress" when it is still too vulnerable to be exposed to the harsh glare of daylight.

I still support and even insist on the creative person's right to have private time during the creative process (more on that later), but it is often a great advantage to have open dialogue with your client while you explore the first murmurs of a creative idea.

The premise we're driving to here is that great work isn't sold in the presentation, it's sold *between presentations,* in those moments when client and agency are working in seamless harmony, focused on a common goal, exchanging points of view without trace of egocentric protectiveness.

During the many years I spent on the Levi's account, my partner and I enjoyed a stimulating proximity to the brand through the intimate relationship we enjoyed with the President of Levi's Canada. Formally and informally, we found ourselves sharing views and throwing around ideas that would often fall to earth months later in the form of a billboard or TV spot.

As far back as the 80s, Chiat\Day in LA continually ran self-initiated focus groups in order to try out new creative ideas for some of their clients. In those instances they would invite the client along to "watch them air their dirty laundry" as one planner put it. It gave the client a ringside seat at a private, potentially embarrassing show, but cleverly, it made the client an emotional stakeholder in the agency's pursuit of brilliance.

One last word on sharing. Good creative people are generally *open people*. By that I mean they're interested in all kinds of stimuli that provide clues to doing great work. If you're not open, you're susceptible to repeating yourself over and over again in your work, and of course that's creative suicide. Ask yourself whether you're truly "creatively open," and if you're not sure of the answer, a great way to find out is to monitor yourself when your client is expressing his or her point of view on your work. If you find yourself shutting down and turning to stone, you need to do some work in this area. You'll be better off for it.

An important note of caution: make sure you're the one where the creative buck stops. You're the one holding the yardstick of the creative standard, make sure you use it. Every client must know that although the ultimate decision as to what runs is theirs, the creative integrity of the work belongs to the creative team.

Making Love with the Lights On

Assuming then that there is a significant amount of support and motivation for the advertising from the very top of the client's organization, and that this influence has filtered through the client's ranks, what about the day-to-day operators of the business on the *agency* side? Where do they fit in?

I had been talking to a group of young creative people about the idea of sharing a creative relationship with their fellow professionals, account management people in particular, when a young copywriter commented that what I was proposing was comparable to making love with the lights on. I understand the need most creative people feel for working in private, and the fear of having too many people, particularly inexperienced people, contaminate the creative idea. This is a fragile issue and I appreciate how this sense of protectiveness can be quite well founded.

The reality is, however, that with the importance clients place on the creative product today, and the consequent burden placed on the shoulders of creative people, this kind of sharing and internal support for the work is often beneficial, and can provide the creative group with the nurturing that aids rather than obstructs.

As a note: if this interdependence is inevitable, it becomes fair for creative people to become more involved in the hiring of those who will work alongside them. Truth is, it has become a right for art directors and writers to demand they interview new account people they'll be working with. It also falls to agency management to become more conscious of group dynamics and interaction, and to assemble account group/creative teams based on their latent compatibility, rather than constructing the group based solely on the perceived client need.

Much of this has begun to happen and the playful animosity that existed between account group and creative in the past has mostly dissipated, most often replaced by a far less territorial working relationship.

All this said, we need to rethink how we find unfettered creative territory for ourselves in this far more exposed, less private place where the lights are on. This need for a sacred and proprietary place is not born out of ego, but out of that natural instinct creative people have for needing to satisfy their own nagging creative voice. It is this original voice inside all of us that carries with it the primal strands and unformed tissue of brave new ideas, and without which the quantum leaps that inspire brilliance can never be made. It's why Gauguin went to Tahiti, Turner to Venice, Byron to Greece.

A Room of One's Own

I had always envisaged the ideal creative playpen to be an entirely white room, with white walls, a white ceiling, and minimal white furniture. Some kind of pristine unsullied space designed to subconsciously induce the mind to free-fall through limitless space into uncharted new territory.

The more I have come to understand the nature of ideas, the more I have come to realize that this wouldn't be the right room at all. To understand what would constitute the right room, one needs first to understand the nature of ideas. What is an idea? What exactly is this elusive grail without which our business and perhaps civilization at large would cease to be?

In the mystical tradition you will find the precept that an idea is the creation of *that which never existed before* and that only *once* in all of creation has that ever happened: in the Act of Creation itself. Since then, all ideas are constituted from elements that have always been around. Unintroduced to the world or to one another, but essentially there from the beginning. (Fire, for example, wasn't new, but rather the introduction of two sticks rubbing against one another to provide the friction necessary to create it.) Simply put, an idea is a way of *connecting old things in a brand new way.* Witness Doyle Dane's famous Volkswagen campaign quoted earlier. The appearance of the word "Lemon" below the car forged an unexpectedly new combination of old elements. Here, the language of advertising, which had customarily used positive, complimentary words to sell its wares, was expressing the surprising opposite. Hence the anatomy of the "Lemon" idea: a car someone wants you to buy, described by an unflattering remark.

What follows then is that the right kind of creative playroom is a room filled with unconnected, unresolved pieces: a spare wheel, fragments of fabric, a door handle, a fork (no knife), a guitar without strings, building blocks, etc. In a room such as this, the creative person would experience a milieu more analogous to the mechanism of mind required to generate ideas—essentially a room that would allow the creative mind to join things to each other, or imagine them as a part of another.

While many agencies provide play areas replete with pool table and pinball machines, the more productive space would be something like the bric-a-brac room described above. Whether your agency offers this kind of space or not, it is vitally important for your creative voice to be given "a room of its own." A place to reflect, sharpen, think, a place to try out bold new ideas, either on one's own or with your creative partner.

If you don't have the privilege of a room, at least find the time to leave the confines of the agency and sit in a park or a coffee shop or anywhere, where some distance lends some sharpness to the view. Particularly now, in this the new environment one is asked to be "creative" in, the requirement to be alone in your creative explorations from time to time preserves the edge of the creative axe made blunt by the wear and tear of daily use.

The Young Are Fast, but the Old Are Accurate

The tilt towards a more involved, business orientation in the agency has inevitably led to a different talent profile within the creative department. The old aphorism that "nobody under the age of 30 is capable of having a good idea" has been invalidated to an extent by the need for marketing maturity that runs deeper than flashes of thirty-second brilliance.

Through what is probably some kind of natural evolutionary process, the talent mix one finds in many creative departments today includes not only the 22-year-old whiz-kid's creative abilities, but the valuable business consciousness and client skills of the seasoned 40-year-old.

This is a time in which there's a new place for so-called older creative people in our agencies. This is not to say that this "older" talent should ever replace the young and the swift. There is an energy and salience brought to the creative product through our young talent that keeps the work feeling contemporary and relevant. It is, and perhaps will always be, a young person's business this way.

However, I do think that an agency that takes into account its client mix, agency culture and product philosophy, and drives it through an appropriate *mix* of youth and maturity in its creative staffing, is not only enjoying the best of both worlds, but is well attuned to the current creative charge.

The rest becomes an issue for the creative director's astute management: the art of applying a constant stir stick to the talent mix and making sure that the proper blend of interchange takes place on a daily basis, to keep the veterans fresh and the blazing young guns firing accurately. Happily, when great work is the simple goal, the hardy creative veteran and the innocent, wide-eyed wunderkind mix rather well.

Unarguably one of North America's premier creative agencies, Fallon McElligott has succeeded wonderfully at amalgamating a tough, grownup mentality with their youthful, creative vigour. As paradoxical as this might appear, what Fallon does is mix *responsibility* with the kind of *irresponsibility* that is most often necessary to accomplishing real creative breakthrough. One particular manifestation of this approach involves the unequivocal encouragement of management to always pursue the creative road less travelled. Should the creative meet with client rejection, the encouragement turns to tough love in which the creative team are allowed a brief period of mourning and then told to get over their defeat and return with something even better. A get-back-on-the-horse philosophy that never accepts defeat.

There is no escaping the fact that this rigour ultimately leads to the question of creative principles and how to protect them in this far more demanding environment. After all is said and done, there is no surer way to protect creative principles than through the sheer refusal to produce anything that doesn't satisfy one's own creative criteria. It's the only effective way. But don't mistake this opposition for the bloody-mindedness of the prima donna era of advertising. The context here is entirely different. This time, the resistance is driven by that deeper, more involved business perspective that should have won the client's respect. You should in most cases find support and understanding from your client when this occurs. (If the client doesn't view your creative stand this way, it's an unfortunate sign that the client/agency relationship needs work.)

The Lost Art of Tunnel Building

There's no part of the process more important to the end product than the creative strategy. While everyone in the business knows this, it's a curious fact that so much strategic development is done with relatively little involvement from the creative team who will execute the thinking.

This has less to do with the strategic ability of creative people and more to do with their apathy. The "waiting for the strategy to get to you" mentality is a leftover from the linear assembly line process of old, an anachronism that must be abandoned if you want to pursue the exceptional solution. Without getting involved in the strategy development, you just won't do the kind of creative that makes clients listen to what you have to say and so buy your work.

The way it seems to operate most often in agencies is that the strategy is developed by the planner and/or the account group and then shown to the creative director and sometimes to the respective creative team simultaneously. Once it passes this stage, it becomes actionable. In my view, this is too late in the process. In the current milieu, it's vital that the creative team directly involved on the business should not just be asked to agree to the strategy, but should be involved in shaping it.

This isn't that complicated. If the creative players are more attuned to the greater context of the work they're doing, their participation in the strategic development becomes natural. *This is important.* The initial strategic discussion, even if it's just scratchings and musings with planners and account people, *needs your attention.*

By nature, the discussion today takes place within a broader 360-

degree context, involving more aspects of the client's business than simply the advertising. I encourage you to bring your perspective to the proceedings. Share your intuitions, even if they're not fully realized. Ask questions about those details that you intuitively feel might have some bearing on the creative task. Above all, push those whose chief responsibility is the strategy to deliver a tighter, simpler, better thought-out document. Every inch is vital. The axiom is true, that an inch of difference in the thinking makes a mile of difference in the execution. That's just the way the metaphysics work.

When the thinking has been done and the creative strategy agreed to, the creative journey begins. While you work with the strategy, stay committed to it, but always, always keep a light burning on the front porch for that unpredictable revelation that can occur when a voracious creative mind goes out hunting.

What we mean by this is that sometimes a flash of brilliance occurs that doesn't fully fit the strategy. An insight that the linear process of strategy development didn't uncover. Whatever you do, don't discard that insight. Albert Einstein said it this way:

> First I come up with the idea and then I come up with the mathematics to justify the idea. If the mathematics don't work, I don't throw out the idea, I throw out the mathematics.

Einstein understood that big ideas are not born of linear formulae (and a creative strategy is essentially a formula for communication), but through nonlinear leaps. But be careful: this is not an excuse for ignoring the strategy and retrofitting some postscript thinking to your creative solution. It's more about extracting the strategic insight embedded in your revelation, and returning it to the greater context of the original strategy, to help reorder or rethink the elements in that document.

Try to be open to a process in which there is constant dialogue between the creative group and the account/strategy leaders as the work takes shape. Each party should try to stay open to incorporating the insightful, even if only nuanced, changes that the other brings to the building process.

As noted elsewhere, there has always been a divide between the language of creativity and that of strategy. In a process such as the one described here, you will find the silos of separation naturally disappear, to be replaced by something more akin to the art of tunnel building. Namely, the collaboration of two separate parties who begin in opposite places but chip away towards one another, ultimately meeting in the middle when the last wall is broken.

Why Is the Man Standing on His Head?

Let us return to Koestler's point about originality being the very essence of creativity, for there is arguably no place more difficult to communicate in an original way than in advertising.

This has much to do with the fact that no other form of communication is burdened to deliver the research-measured criterion of breakthrough the way a print ad or a thirty-second commercial is meant to. If your work doesn't achieve breakthrough norms, the client simply won't run it, and justifiably so. Advertising costs too much not to be noticed.

Now, breakthrough has everything to do with *one's ability to surprise:* the capacity to make a viewer say, *"Gee, I've never seen anything like this before,"* and in so doing arrest attention long enough for the ad to go to work and sell the product. Lamentably, surprise in this day and age is more difficult to achieve than ever. Each time a television camera takes us live to a previously unimaginable disaster, a bizarre courtroom drama, an AIDS hospital for children, a President refuting sex charges, the notion of what is truly surprising is redefined. The question of how to *show someone who's seen everything, something they're never seen before,* is now, more than ever, the underlying challenge for the creative mind employed in advertising.

It is because of this crucial need to surprise that so much bad advertising gets made. And it's bad for the obvious reason that surprise without *relevance,* either to the product or to the consumer, is an unforgivable corruption of our craft. I am not suggesting that this kind of waste is new or that it is merely the result of the proliferation of shocking images beamed at us by CNN. The tension between being original and being relevant has always been a central one in advertising, and no chapter about creative responsibility should forget to reaffirm the absolute need for relevance and originality to be, always and forever, faithful bedfellows.

Too much work gets to market without being relevant. Equally, too much work gets to market without being surprising. All too often, the surprising aspect of the work has been stripped away until it is not much more than the comfortable familiarity that focus groups are wont to approve. Like hearing the same joke told again. And that too is a dreadful waste of money.

No matter how much you're in love with your latest ad, before you venture forth from your office clasping the page in your hand, listen to the small voice inside you that asks whether your brilliance has relevance.

Remember Bernbach's integrity when (in his words) he remarked, "I wouldn't show a man standing on his head, except if I was advertising a suit with special pockets that stopped money from falling out." What he was saying is, ask yourself always, *why is the man in my ad standing on his head?*

When You Get to the Dance, Dance with the One Who Brought You.

You are now at the production stage: a crossing that can be both taxing and exhilarating as the many newcomers necessary to the process begin to contribute their talents. In producing print advertising, the introduction of photographers and illustrators, print production managers and the like means that there are now new godfathers and mothers of what has been, until now, your baby. In producing a television commercial, producers, directors, cameramen, editors, musicians, and talent, both behind and in front of the camera, are now hired to help give the idea flesh and form.

It is important to allow these people into the process, rather than keeping them at a controlled distance. It is vital they understand what you are trying to accomplish beyond what is apparent on the storyboard. Consider allowing them some discretionary insight into the strategic objective of the message if you think it might help provide added direction and clarity. This kind of sharing instills a subliminal sense of trust that encourages the very best effort from all concerned.

Staying true to the idea throughout the production is paramount. It can be taxing to ward off well-meaning directors whose embellishments are diluting the idea rather than strengthening it, but these confrontations are necessary and well worth having. This said, you will be impressed by the vantage point of those who are new to the idea—the objectivity of the musical composer or the film editor who senses a pertinent layer or angle that might have escaped you.

As noted earlier, try to stay open. But balance your openness with a dogged protectiveness of the idea. Develop the astuteness necessary to keeping the inapt at bay while allowing access to relevant improvement.

While in the production phase, the axiom to keep in mind is this one: *the brand is everything and everything is the brand.* Every tool you use will either accrue to the brand's desired properties or devalue them. The talent you choose, the music you use, the look of the film, etc. are all critically important, and must provide relevant embellishment to the central idea. Make sure you measure the use of each with the proper consideration. Don't use a director whose style is antithetical to the strategic idea—e.g. one who prefers low angles, fast cutting, and flashy sets, when the brand personality is all about sincerity, simplicity, and substance. Don't use dark, murky backgrounds and busy typefaces in a print ad for a dish detergent whose brand promise is clean, white, sparkling dishes. Even while engaged in the production, stay close to the brand strategy. You owe it to yourself, the hard path you've travelled to get here, and the client you're doing it for.

A Word on Career Management

Whether you're searching for your first job in advertising or looking to move up to a new opportunity, managing your career is now as much about keeping your creative skills honed, as it is about amassing some strategic ability.

Today, being able to show how the work in your portfolio either sparked the thinking or dramatized it is a key requisite of a marketable skill-set. Simply being able to discuss strategic thinking in your interview will already begin to set you apart from other candidates in a job search.

One of the more impressive portfolios I've seen from a creative person included a copy of the strategy (printed and pasted alongside the ad) with some annotations she'd made on the strategy sheet that indicated where she thought clues to the creative solution lay waiting. There were also underlines and question marks on the page, signalling where she perceived the strengths and gaps lay in the thinking. Whether these were real or faux, added as drama for the interviewer's benefit, didn't matter to me. The effect worked. The same person brought along letters of reference from clients she had worked with: a smart way to demonstrate her ability to build solid client relationships.

This is the kind of portfolio the current climate requires, and it is a show of currency that has real value to a potential employer. Whatever you do, please don't include a pile of work under the heading "this is how brilliant I am but the client wasn't smart enough to buy it." There are a hundred good ads being made all over the industry every day that don't survive. They are the unfortunate and inevitable roadkill of our business.

Concentrate on filling your book and your interview with the kind of maturity that not only demonstrates how good your game is, but as importantly, how well you understand *the playing field*.

Proactivity Is Fun, Reactivity Is Exhausting

The business of advertising has become extremely complex and in many ways has lost direction. Affected by the daily turbulence its clients endure, the modern advertising agency seeks traction in a rapidly changing communication landscape while pursuing growth and delivering profitability.

This chapter in dedicated to the belief that the future of our business, as it always has, lies in the complete dedication of the agency to its clients' business—but the *nature* of that dedication must change. In my view it is the creative mind, with all the expanded sensibilities I have attempted to describe here (even if that mind doesn't live in the creative department), that must lead that change.

The word "fun" is seldom used to describe what we do everyday in our jobs in advertising. It was a word last used to describe the double-martini-for-lunch era that is now gone forever. Fun in the future will come from our proactive, whole-hearted creative involvement. Its opposite—the exhausting, endless reactivity that has forced many of us back on our heels—must become a thing of the past for the business we're in to be more meaningful and fulfilling.

Without that deep down satisfaction (as an old advertising cliché might put it) the talent so critical to making this industry a vibrant and imaginative one will migrate elsewhere. Or worse, that original voice that might have grown up to be Bernbach will never be heard.

Overview: Chapter Six

At one time, I was the Course Leader at a weeklong offsite. The theme was how to get more effective advertising. There were about twenty marketing people, half of them men and half of them women. They were there to hear top speakers from various agencies.

In one session, a Creative Director, almost in passing, mentioned to the group that it was in their interest to motivate creative people. Four Brand Managers, all men as it happened, were sitting side by side along one side of the U-shaped table. Their arms snapped into the folded position—classic male body language of disagreement. They challenged the idea with some intensity, along the lines of "nobody goes out of their way to motivate me, so why should I go out of my way to motivate you." The meeting went through an awkward moment.

This chapter reasserts that it is absolutely in the manager's interest to motivate creative people, coming down to the most powerful reason of all. It leads to better work.

Chapter Six

Working with Creative People

RUPERT BRENDON

Introduction

My father was an advertising copywriter and novelist, and my brother is a much-published author, so I discovered early on that creative people march to a different drummer. During my career—which has gone from account management to agency management to my current ICA position—I've seen clients and colleagues (myself included on occasion) struggle with how best to handle this.

Every relationship is different, but there is broad agreement on the major do's and don'ts. This chapter will try to capture them.

Sources

I've discussed this question extensively with client and agency colleagues over the years, and read widely on the topic.[1] I've also drawn on various publications (see the bibliography) and my own experience.

An Anecdote

A senior client was looking at an ad layout, and had brought a junior along for the experience. The Writer and Art Director were senior. The

---

[1] There have been a number of common themes, and I'm not able to trace everything back to original sources. Colleagues will recognize thoughts they have given me at various times, and I thank them for their ideas here.

Account Director had set up the purpose of the meeting. The Account Executive was there for followup. The senior client had been well trained in how to raise "concerns." Towards the end of the discussion, modulating his voice to be firm but constructive, he says, "I just have one more question—it's about the size of the logo." Quick as a flash, the Art Director says, "I can make it smaller if you like." This story gets a good laugh, and it sets up what we are going to cover:

a) It confirms that it matters how you position things to creative people.
b) It looks like a committee—not a good forum for discussing ideas.
c) It illustrates that the "world view" of people is often different.
d) It's another example of creative people seeing things with a twist.
e) It shows the value of the lighter touch.

The Target Audience for This Chapter

My audience is Account Management at agencies, and Marketing/Management at clients. I hope that creative people also read this, of course. The message is this:

> The effort to create the productive working relationship[2] must come primarily—some say exclusively—from the management side.

It may stir the sinews to see something this one-sided but it's a fact of life. Creative people may be a delight or a nightmare to work with, but "building a relationship" is way down their priority list, if it's there at all.

The Creative Person

Everyone is creative up to a point, as theorists and educators earnestly remind us, but that's too broad for our purpose. There are also different types of creativity. I doubt if Buckminster Fuller or Henry Moore or Picasso could have written an ad campaign.

---

2 Note that it says "productive" working relationship, not "comfortable" or "easy-going" or even "friendly."

I can't see Margaret Atwood dashing off a snappy line—though apparently Salman Rushdie did. He reputedly came up with a marvelous line for cream cakes, "Naughty. But Nice." Then there is scientific creativity ("How's that relativity idea coming, Albert?") and inventor's creativity—the sort that brought us Velcro and Post-It Notes.

One of the first people to study creativity was Arthur Koestler.[3] He describes it as taking two things seemingly unrelated, and fusing them together (the bi-sociative act), as in the Archimedes story. The King thinks he has been swindled. He wants to know if his crown is pure gold, without snipping a piece off. Archimedes is puzzling over this as he gets into the tub. The water rises. The next thing we know, he's running naked down the street. He has suddenly seen how to measure the volume of the crown, and with that he can tell if it is pure gold.

Most of us have had this feeling (though not to the extent of going streaking). It was behind Velcro and Post-It Notes. It is what brainstorming tries to unlock. It is at work when "insights" are uncovered. And it is behind many great advertising campaigns.

It's important to realize that "bi-sociation" isn't the only type of creativity, of course. It is not a big part of Shakespeare's plays or Leonardo's painting or Mozart's music, for example. But people who are above-averagely creative do have an innate ability *to see things in a different way.* Anyone in business might have this ability, but here we are talking about the people in the creative department—and by extension their colleagues in the world of production.

Are Creative People Different?

Creative people have two abilities more than others. They see things in new ways. And they have talent. These are related, but they are not the same. Talent is the ability to do things much better than average. The three tenors at singing. Randy Johnson at pitching. Van Gogh at painting sunflowers. Talent does not necessarily make a person creative, though talent and creativity often go together.[4]

---

3 See *The Act of Creation* in the bibliography.
4 The distinction is captured in Winston Fletcher's *Tantrums and Talent.*

The ability to see things in new ways relates to how the brain is wired, and creative people are more right-brained than average.[5]

Left Brain	Right Brain
Logical, Linear, Verbal, Analytical, Focused. Needs things to make sense. Wants to find the one right answer.	Intuitive, Lateral, Visual, Spatial, Conceptual. Not troubled by paradoxes. Explores anything. Not looking for a "right answer."
[Left Brain] thinking chooses, looks for what is right, maintains that one thing must follow directly from another, concentrates on relevance, and moves in the most likely direction.	*Lateral [Right Brain] thinking changes, looks for what is different, makes deliberate jumps, welcomes chance intrusions, and explores the least likely.*
Edward de Bono	Edward de Bono

Many great campaigns reflect this, and are based on making something "the least likely" work brilliantly. My favourite is "Manhattan Landing." The fact that British Airways flies a lot of people across the Atlantic hardly makes the heart beat a little faster. The Island of Manhattan, screaming onto a runway at Heathrow, certainly does.

It's fair to say that a lot of creative people are not as strong as their account management and client colleagues in some left brain areas, and vice versa.[6]

Broader than this, though, is whether creative people have a different approach to life and work. The answer is yes. A "right brain" view of life is not at all the same as a "left brain" view, as this quote shows:

For creative people, their work isn't what they do. It's who they are.

---

5 Left Brain-Right Brain theory is not as simple as "left" and "right," but this is close enough for our purposes.

6 A tip to creative people. You may find left-brain responses frustrating, but you won't win people over by saying, "You're too analytical." They owe much of their success to analytical ability, and do not react well if you portray it as a weakness.

Let's look at the implications of this for the manager.[7]

Two World Views

In creative matters the terms "art" and "science" often come up. I've never liked this distinction because art, in the purest sense, is not commercial—and nor is science. However, two world views do exist:

The "Business" View	The "Creative" View
We all know why we're here. Advertising is a tool to do a job. I want the best, most effective, tool for doing that job.	The best way to reach people is to touch them in ways they have never been touched before. That's what I do.

These two views *can be very close*—as they have been for Nike and others. But they can also be a long way apart, especially on the question of what "best, most effective" entails. If the world views are adamantly in conflict, you could be facing what the marriage counselors call irreconcilable differences. Happily, this is rare, and you can set about creating a motivated and productive environment, while handling differences constructively and positively.

Creating the Right Environment

Red Adair is world expert at putting out oil well fires. If your oil well is ablaze you make it as easy as possible for him to do his job. When it comes to getting work out of agencies the same principle applies.

Create an "odds-on" environment for the creative people.

Some of you will think, "They get paid enough. Why do I have to worry about this?" If this bell has chimed, it's hard to un-ring it. I can only tell you that every shred of advice is the same—if you don't make it *your* job to create the right environment, you will not get the best work, and top creative people will not want to work on your business.

---

7 I'm calling marketing and account people "managers" from here on.

The right environment, from a creative point of view, is where all play-ers want breakthrough ideas—and embrace the risk that goes along with this. In helping create this environment, it helps to know how ideas happen. We've all had ideas out of the blue, but this is only half the story. Bertrand Russell, the British philosopher and mathematician, put it like this:

> Having, by a time of very intense concentration, planted the problem in my subconscious, it would germinate underground until, suddenly, the solution emerged with blinding clarity, so that it only remained to write down what had happened as if in a revelation.

Edison had his famous 1% inspiration, 99% perspiration comment, and Louis Pasteur said the same thing in another way, "Chance favours the prepared mind."

This is why a good briefing is so important. This is also why creative people need incubation time before the best ideas occur. With the speed of business today we often don't allow for this. There's even a "just in time" mentality in the air. While it's true that ideas—on occa-sion even very good ones— can occur under impossible deadlines, this is not an "odds on" environment. The best managers make sure the schedule has breathing room for creative development.[8]

Another issue is how ideas are treated. The left brain is quick to judgment. In many fields of business this is admirable. But not when looking at ideas. This led to the following quote from the father of brainstorming:

> All ideas are born drowning. (Attributed to Alex Osborn.)

Good managers understand this. They don't seize on what they may see as flaws. They create "room" for ideas to grow. They also under-stand why some creative people are reluctant, to the point of paranoia, to show work in progress.

---

8 It's true that many creative people procrastinate—understandable, given how often their ideas run into a buzz-saw of concerns. But they can't help notice that "strategy" and "research" seem to get a more generous slice of the pie when schedules are being put together. They have a point.

Finally, there's overall ambience. Don't be puritanical. This is not a licence for irresponsibility (many creative environments have been extremely hard-driving). It's just a reminder to have a sense of humour.

Handling the Paradoxes

There are a lot of these with creative people. Some managers have a knack for handling them. Others have to learn how. But left-brain logic will not make them go away. Let's look at the main ones.

1. *"I wasn't put on this planet to do that."*

> The best creative people are utterly committed to what they do. So, we might suppose they would also be passionate about "moving boxes off the shelf."
>
> A few are, and some (out of courtesy to clients) fan the embers of their interest, but the majority don't look at things this way. They are passionate about the art, skill, guile, craft, sheer out-of-the-boxness of getting a message across in an utterly new and ingenious way.[9] That's why a company with a tried-and-true attitude to creative does not raise the pulse rate of creative people, even if it is the biggest and richest company on the planet.
>
> The quote above came from a top creative director, asked to pool out a successful but creatively pedestrian campaign. A client who wants to pool out a winning formula will sometimes demand top talent, but oddly enough that does not get the best work. Some people a right for the challenge of pooling out a campaign. Some aren't. It's better to take a horses-for-courses approach.
>
> Think about how you would pick an architect. You want the person most in tune with the task at hand. Frank Lloyd Wright was brilliant, but he probably would not have been right for redesigning an extension to your house.

---

9 Yes, it also has to be relevant, and it has to work.

2. *Attitude to Direction*

Agencies work to a direction defined by some combination of positioning, creative strategy, and creative briefing. The manager needs to remember, though, that the creative mind doesn't *innately* work in such a disciplined way. It tends to resist orders.[10]

Yes, it's true that some of the world's great artistic achievements follow "orders," and you can point to Shakespeare's iambic pentameters, Milton's sonnets, Bach's counterpoint, haiku, and similar examples.

But creative people usually arrive at the great idea only after meandering through minefields of half-buried possibilities. Some managers feel this is inefficient, and try to head it off. This finger wagging is a real downer. The solution comes from Norman Berry, at one time a top Creative Director in the UK and on Madison Avenue:

Give me the freedom of a tightly defined strategy.

He points out that if you are doggedly restrictive you will not inspire the team, but if you give carte blanche you confront them with the tyranny of the blank page. With the WHAT very clearly defined, and the HOW open, they can explore the limitless possibilities that lead to great ideas.

3. *Praise and Flattery*

Kenneth Tynan was a feared and admired critic. He said, "A critic is a man who knows the way, but can't drive the car." Most performers give critics short shrift ("If they were any good, they'd be performing themselves") but still care what they say. I don't recall where praise is in Maslow's pyramid, but we all need it, and creative people need it more that most—because their work is part of themselves.

---

10 Creative Strategy has always had two objectives (1) to define WHAT is to be said but also (2) in the words of P&G, "to keep the creative effort on track."

When giving praise, your personality comes play. If you do it naturally and genuinely, that's very good. If you find it hard, then you have to learn how to do it well, even though you may feel uncomfortable for a while. Parsimonious praisers feel false. They feel they are "just saying it." These are the same people who, when asked if they give feedback to their people, say, "They know how I feel." But lack of communication is very demotivating. A little flattery is fine, provided you don't lay it on with a trowel. Generous praisers might do this a little more than some pursed-lipped bean-counter would condone, but it works wonders.

Alex Osborn saw creativity as a flower that bloomed when nourished with praise. We all do better work if our efforts are appreciated. So if you are a parsimonious praiser, loosen up.

4. *Prima Donnas*

Leo Burnett (who wore expensive but rumpled suits, and was decidedly un-stylish) was in the elevator when a gaggle of his creative staff, outlandishly dressed in every way, clattered in. As he got off, he was heard to mutter, "You'd better be _____ good!"

Managers don't like prima donnas, but genuine prima donnas *are* good—think of Maria Callas. Sadly, some creative folk milk the stereotype. Most of the time, as with Callas, it's in your interest to accommodate talent. But you don't want to kowtow to a pretender. You can use your own judgment to tell the difference, of course. This is also one of reasons to have friends in the creative community. They can give you the scoop. What about the creative people who are easy to work with? If they produce great work, thank your lucky stars. But be guided by the work, not the comfort factor.

5. *Whose Money Is It Anyway?*

Suppose you are disagreeing with a creative team. As a client, the money question may cross your mind. Do not say it out loud. The disagreement comes from the difference in world views. They are still telling you what they believe is right. Resolve the disagreement as productively as you can,[11] but don't use money as a big stick. It won't help.

---

11 But not by compromise. See comments on handling disagreement in Chapter 8.

The Pecking Order

Clients are looking for the most effective and ingenious ways to build their brands. Agencies exist because they add something over and above what clients can do for themselves—creativity.[12] This makes the creative role special.

On the other side of the coin, however, is the question of the coin. Clients look at who is footing the bill, and don't respond well to the inference (yes, it happens) that creative people see themselves as higher up on some imaginary pecking order. Do these cross-currents exist, and if so, what does the good manager do about them? Charles de Gaulle had a philosophy, "Exploit the inevitable."

Creative people know they are in a service business, and that clients will have the last say. But, as in the story of Michaelangelo and the Sistine Chapel, they feel it is their right and responsibility to tell the Pope what to do.

If you feel this happening, don't get ruffled. Most of the time the cross-currents relate back to the two world views. Think about how you feel on the rare occasions your work is held up before a group and critiqued. Then imagine this happening with everything you produce. Handle the cross-currents with grace. They are part of the fun of swimming in challenging waters. [13]

Risk and Responsibility

This is the title of an old training video from the UK. A creative director presents the Hathaway eye-patch ad to two account people.[14] With uncanny predictability, they are full of praise, and then raise their concerns. The final one is about "that thing," the eye-patch. It worries them on two fronts: (a) it takes advantage of a disability, and (b) it associates Hathaway with an unpleasant eye disease.

---

12 This creativity applies in the broadest sense, not just "the ad campaign."

13 Once in a while a cross-current becomes a dangerous undertow. This is not acceptable, and has to be dealt with face to face, or by bringing higher management into the picture.

14 In terms of what they say, the account people could equally well have been clients. This tape is still floating around, and is worth trying to track down.

The ad launched one of the most famous campaigns in history. But in the video the account people think the concerns are "responsible," in relation to the "risk." The eye-patch is removed, and the ad is averaged down into safe obscurity.

There is a similar exercise showing how the "Think Small" VW Beetle campaign could have been reduced to rubble. And imagine the concerns—all sensible on the surface—that could have killed Apple's 1984 ad. IBM is equated to Big Brother, and IBM users (who Apple were targetting) are shown as mindless zombies.[15]

These examples illustrate something that can be tough to come to grips with:

The attempt to eliminate risk can frequently create it.

This is a touchy subject, because "risk" is loaded. Opportunity and excitement to one person are irresponsibility and danger to another. It would help enormously if English had a word for "right risk." It doesn't, but here's a way to assess it:

The Odds of Success × The Reward

outweigh

The Odds of Failure × The Consequences

All the great breakthrough ideas carried risk. In approving such work, it helps immensely if you have a high-risk threshold. But if you don't, think about *all* the risks, including the risk of making something so "safe" that it becomes wallpaper.

Creative people and managers often see risk differently. We can't cover all the possibilities here. I would, however, like to touch on three:

---

15 Apparently, focus group research raised red flags, but Apple went ahead anyway—a reminder about the need to *interpret,* and sometimes ignore, what "research says."

1. *The Tried and True Scenario*

Suppose you are convinced that the best plan is to continue with a tried and true campaign—and that even to *consider a* new approach is risky. It can be frustrating or irritating if the creative people want to explore new ideas anyway.

This is a clash of world views. Creative people *always* believe there is a new, different and better solution out there—it just has to be discovered. They may be right, but you may still not want to take the risk of coming up empty. Whoever is "right," it is better if you are empathetic, not judgmental.

2. *The Bacon & Eggs Scenario*

An agency recommended something that the client thought put his career on the line. After listening patiently he said, "Ah, the bacon & eggs scenario." Puzzled looks drew the explanation. "With bacon & eggs, the chicken makes a contribution, but the pig makes a life and death commitment." If clients feel they are going to be in harm's way, it's the agency's turn to be empathetic.

3. *The "Consumer Won't Get It" Scenario*

Most consumers don't frequent the symphony, or the ballet, or art galleries, or museums. They don't read what the literati say is good literature. They may not be on top of current affairs. They don't belong to Mensa. This has led to two schools of thought about creative. One is that when it comes to their self-interest, consumers are *smart.* They may not be intellectuals, but they put 2 and 2 together to make 4. This is Bernbach's view—based on charm, wit, irony, an unexpected idea, and a devout belief that you don't browbeat customers into submission.

The other school is less optimistic about consumers. This is the school of "tell 'em what you want to tell 'em." Creative people tend to be Bernbachian. Client and Account Management people vary. There are successes (and failures) in both camps. If you want to get the best out of someone in the opposite camp, it's a good idea to reach a meeting of the minds.

Tunnel Vision

The consumer gives advertising only a split second of attention, yet we can spend months of tortuous effort to get them to that moment. All of us get caught up in this. I know of a long debate about which way the bears should dance around the Sugar Crisp bowl. We can smile, but most of us have been there.

Here's a true story. The President of Company A never got involved with advertising. One year, out of the blue, he asked for a meeting with the agency "to learn more about advertising." The agency and marketing group wondered what this could be about. They settled on having an informal discussion, based on the agency's work for Company A and other clients. One of these was Company B.

It so happened that the agency had been in a struggle with Company B. The agency wanted to lighten up the Brand Character in B's advertising, but the client wasn't sure. Only after months of tense meetings, and a lot of research, did they finally agree to take what they saw as a big image risk. They were very worried about the creative that had gone on air.

It turned out that President A wanted to send a message to his marketing department. He thought A's advertising should be more like B's! (He was in B's target audience, by the way.) Meanwhile, Company B was telling the agency that they admired their work for Company A. This is just one story, but it illustrates the tunnel vision that we all have to some degree:

> The way we look at our own advertising is utterly different from the way we look at someone else's.

Consumers don't do this, of course. So what may loom large to us may be just a nice change to them. A way to put this in perspective is to look at admirable campaigns that have worked. In a high percentage of Cassies cases the winning brand could have succumbed to tunnel vision. Read the cases and imagine you were there at the time. Imagine the concerns. See how they were outweighed by the opportunity. In other words, assess for yourself how they took the right risk.[16]

---

16 There are now over 100 cases at www.cassies.ca, with the accumulated learning captured in David Rutherford's "Crossover Notes." The Cassies launched in 1993, when some colleagues and I saw the need for awards that reflect effectiveness. The Cassies are modeled on the IPA Effectiveness Awards in the UK. Success is based on proven results, validated by a rigorous business case, signed off by client and agency management, and judged by top professionals from all disciplines.

Earning Respect

These seem to be the keys to success for the manager:

- *Having high standards.* As Chiat said, "Good enough is not good enough."
- *Handling the difference in world views.*
- *Believing in creative.* Some ideas work spectacularly, some fail, and some are in the middle. Deal with this in a "half-full" way. Naïve optimism doesn't earn respect, but nor does diligent pessimism.
- *Fighting for ideas.* Put yourself on the line.
- *Having good instincts.* These develop in a number of ways, but perhaps the simplest is to be genuinely interested in how creative is developed, and what it can do. Know the great campaigns. Read cases. Learn from the market and from others.
- *Being good at your job.* This may seem self-evident, but creative people know that if the business is not well run their job will be a lot harder.
- *Not being a pushover.* Even the best creative teams can miss the mark, and not realize it. When you point out that the work needs to be better (and it is a good call) your stature goes up.
- *Listening.* Live by the maxim, "I may disagree with what you say, but I will defend with my life your right to say it."
- *Letting go.* If you are in a position of power you can be a Golda Meier. After a tough discussion, she would say, "Let's be reasonable. Let's do it my way." This will not get the best creative. There are countless decisions that come down to a judgment call. Let some go cheerfully, and agree with the creative point of view.

Handling Disagreements

This will have a profound effect on your ability to get great work. Let's assume you have good judgment about when to take a stand. How should you do it?

- Be constructive, cordial, positive, and patient.[17]
- Remember that you are critiquing something deeply personal.
- Talk in terms of objectives.
- Stick to the big picture.
- Give reasons, but don't be overly analytical.
- Give the creative people a chance to respond. Many concerns are solvable.
- If you feel creative people are defensive, don't say so. It's inflammatory. Of course they will defend their work.
- Don't turn the discussion into a debating contest.[18]
- Don't look for compromise if this will weaken the idea.
- Don't be adversarial. It's not the end of the world if you agree to disagree.
- Look for the baby, not the bathwater.
- Having listened, be decisive.

Things Not to Say

Managers say things (often with good intentions) that come across wrongly.[19] See if any of the following sound familiar:

- **We're looking for a real breakthrough here.** This is great if it is true, but it has come to mean "breakthrough-without-risk." There's nothing wrong with risk avoidance—just ask the people who lost a fortune on the dot.coms—but be candid about it.

---

17 See *Tantrums and Talent*: "Putting errant creators right involves huge amounts of time, argument, resolution and guts."

18 Creative people are not always the best debaters, even when advocating their own ideas. It is the idea that matters, not the ability to debate it.

19 The same is true the other way, but the good manager takes this in stride.

- *I'm not trying to be creative, but...* There are two things wrong with this. First, you *are* trying to be creative. Worse, it's a cliché. Find a more inventive way to get your idea across. In your own words, you might say something like, "I don't think you'll offer me a job, but let me give you an example...."
- *This reminds me of... (as a good thing).* Sometimes an idea has an echo of another. You know it worked, so you see this as good. But how does this sound to someone who lives and breathes by coming up with *new* ideas? If you notice a resemblance, take encouragement from it, but don't mention it.
- *This reminds me of... (as a problem).* You have to mention this. But how you do it makes a big difference. Many of the great ideas in history sprang up in different places almost simultaneously.[20] Some ideas are subconsciously influenced by others. And, though remote, there's the possibility of plagiarism.[21] The tension goes up in this situation, so it's best to raise the similarity as a question, not as a shot across the bow.
- *Let me be devil's advocate for a moment.* From a left-brain point of view, this is perfectly sensible—after all, if an idea can't stand cross-examination, perhaps it isn't very good. But this comment is rarely said constructively, and almost always precedes an attack. Given that "all ideas are born drowning," this is very demotivating.
- *I want to congratulate everybody on all the hard work.* As with the "breakthrough" comment, this would be fine if it meant what it said. But it has come to mean, "Oh my god, they've done all this work and I haven't seen anything that's on the money." It's obviously not ideal if you feel this way. As a first step, assume that there is something—it just hasn't been explained well enough—and ask to be taken through the creative again. You may see something that you did not see before. Then, if you really haven't seen anything, say so in a cordial and constructive way, without the congratulation.
- *Is everybody comfortable?* Think about it. This seemingly innocent question is an invitation to average ideas down into safeness and sameness.

---

20 The telephone, television, and calculus are all examples.
21 Intentional plagiarism is remote for the brutally pragmatic reason that it is likely to be found out. This would ruin a creative person's reputation.

Here's a selection of other comments with a less-than-inspiring effect:

- *It's against policy.*
- *It's all right in theory.*
- *It's too risky.*
- *It'll never work.*
- *They'll never go for it.*
- *We've never done it that way.*
- *It's too clever.*
- *Let's leave this one up to research.*
- *I thought we agreed that we were doing...*
- *If it's so good, how come no one has come up with it before?*
- *Yes, but...*
- *Is it on strategy? (When the real reason is that you just aren't comfortable.)*
- *I'm just not comfortable.*
- *We'll get back to you.*

Awards

Most creative people love awards.[22] Some managers share this enthusiasm, but many don't. What's the best way to handle it when you are on the "against" side?

The first question is: do you want creative people who believe in awards on your business? If you don't, there's no problem. Make your views known, and attract the people (there are some) who share your view. If you want the others, you have a decision to make. You can keep your views to yourself, though they will usually be evident anyway. Or, you can see the issue through the eyes of creative people.

They want to produce something that works, but while doing this, they want to create something wonderfully new, something that sends shivers down the spine—and for that (sorry about this) they value the judgment of their peers more than they value yours. Is that so bad?

The awards advocates also have other points worth considering:

---

22 I am talking about creative awards shows.

- The IPA awards in the UK, and the Cassies, have many effectiveness winners that are highly creative.
- Donald Gunn, and Leo Burnett, have analyzed the winners in top award shows—using business performance. Although not as rigorous as the IPA and Cassies, this effort nevertheless showed a distinct correlation between creative award-winners and in-market success.
- On a broader level, advertising is an increasing intrusion. We used to crash in with the crassest of messages, and that school of thought still exists to some extent. But over the long haul, what will this do to advertising? It will make it increasingly unwelcome.

Awards also tie back to the two world views. It all depends on the type of work you want. As one of Canada's top creative directors said, "Bad work can work, but why would you want to settle for that."

The Creative Presentation

We decided that we would not go into "How to do a Presentation" because this is something agencies should work out with their clients. There are some overall points worth considering, however. As before, I'll start with an anecdote.

A client and agency got together for a presentation. There were five clients in the room, representing three levels, and five agency people. The Account Director said grace by reciting the strategy, and the Account Executive handed out the scripts. The Writer and Art Director looked on, with fixed smiles. The presentation then passed to them. As they started talking, all the clients, in unison, picked up their pens! The reason? A Pavlovian expectation that the creative would need changing.

I urge clients and agencies to discuss this at a very senior level. Are clients optimistic before a presentation? Are agencies optimistic about how clients will react? Given all the effort, how often is the creative right first time? Not often enough.

We need to ask ourselves if a subconscious expectation has crept in: *that it's unlikely a presentation will be followed by dancing in the streets.* I realize this opens Pandora's box, because clients can say, "we would approve it if you would present it," with the agency thinking "but you don't!" It is in all our interests to get beyond this.

In talking this through with client and agency colleagues, the stated expectations are positive, but the privately held views are often not. The attitude seems to be, "Hope for the best. Prepare for the worst." It has to be in everybody's interest to create *an expectation of success.* With this in mind, here are some suggestions:

- Ask clients what works best. Some love a big production. Others actively don't. Some don't want a presentation in the conventional sense at all.[23]
- Tell the agency even if they don't ask. You might like the meeting to start with a review of the strategic thinking, or you may drum your fingers during such an elaborate set up. If you like creative teams to explain about how they arrived at their ideas, encourage this. If you don't, let it be known.[24] If you want the agency to identify "the advertising idea" make this clear. And so on.
- Be candid about expectations, and make the meeting as relaxed as possible. Clients don't like the feeling of being sold, but they want to see enthusiasm and commitment. Agencies hope for spontaneous approval—but many clients don't respond that way.
- To agencies, have some empathy for how clients react to creative. They know about "be yourself" and "be the audience" but this is not so easy when there are several levels of bosses, either in the room or lying in wait outside.
- To clients, find a way to *respond.* Think about when you have given someone a special gift. How do you feel when you get no reaction?
- To senior clients, make it okay for your people to go out on a limb. It's rare for people to say, "I think this is fantastic." Far more common is the furrowed brow and the carefully couched concern.
- This brings up the custom of juniors responding first. When they raise concerns, as they often do, the meeting becomes Pythonesque. The agency rushes to the ramparts. Everyone gets in their two-cents' worth. Suddenly, you have a pitched battle over what could well be a minor point.

---

23 Arthur Fleischmann talks to this point in his chapter on Creative Briefing.
24 Do this privately with the Account Director, and allow for the fact that some creative people need to do this as a kind of ice breaking.

The solution is *not* to put juniors in this position. The trial by fire has some value, but not nearly enough to outweigh the damage. [25] And to agencies, do *not* rush to the ramparts. Park the point politely, and redirect the meeting to the senior clients, getting their response to the creative as a whole.

- Consider introducing tissue sessions. The thinking goes like this. In the classic system, the agency unveils a recommendation at the big presentation. Given that truly breakthrough ideas are *rare*, some present only one solution. Most clients, however, find this too black and white, and want to see alternatives. This has evolved into the "three option" presentation, with clients running easy-to-win side bets on which one will be recommended.

  Whether with one solution or three, however, the agency is "selling" and the client (hopefully) is buying. The ideas may be at a high level of finish. All is well if the client approves the work. But if not, we all know the difficulties.

  Tissue sessions bring the client in earlier, when creative possibilities are germinating, but are not yet fleshed out. They are recognizable as *ideas*, but are a long way from being fully crafted. New or risky or unexpected ideas can be discussed without a "selling" atmosphere. The advantages are obvious. The disadvantage is that although most people believe they can understand ideas in this form, tissues are not the easiest things in the world to assess.[26]

A final point to complete the list. The people in a presentation often have very different personalities. Some of these are naturally compatible with each other, and some are not. You are probably aware of the Myers-Briggs scales that assess personalities along the dimensions of Extravert, Introvert, Sensing, Thinking, Intuiting, Feeling. Along similar lines, the US consultant Stuart Sanders has analyzed scores of presentations, and concluded that clients (as individuals) fall into four broad groupings.[27] Given that everyone wants a successful end result, it is worth being aware—as a team—of the compatibility pitfalls, and running the presentation so that they do not get in the way.

---

25 See E. Peter Elwood on this topic in Chapter 2.

26 Ideas can and do get killed—remember "all ideas are born drowning." This has be handled with great care.

27 This is proprietary, but you can get a sense of it at sandersconsulting.com.

Signs That You Are Getting It Right

There are a number of signs that a manager is getting it right, but I'd like to sum up with just four:

- Talented people want to work on your business.
- They share ideas with you—even when they are not fleshed out.
- They say, "You get it."
- Great work happens on your watch.

When I was at DMB&B we produced Pocket Pieces on various topics. They were aimed at clients, but they apply equally well to Account Management. The one opposite should be a useful summary.

Bibliography

Bedbury, S. (2002). *A New Brand World: 8 Principles for Achieving Brand Leadership in the 21st Century.* New York: Viking.

De Bono, E. (1982). *Lateral Thinking for Management: A Handbook of Creativity.* Toronto: Penguin

De Bono, E. (1987). *Six Thinking Hats.* Markham, ON: Penguin.

Fletcher, W. (1999). *Tantrums and Talent: How to Get the Best from Creative People.* Oxfordshire: Admap.

Foote, C.S. (1996). *The Business Side of Creativity: The Complete Guide for Running a Graphic Design or Communications Business.* New York: Norton.

Kiel, J.M. (1985). *The Creative Mystique: How to Manage It, Nurture It, and Make It Pay.* New York: Wiley.

Koestler, A. (1964). *The Act of Creation.* London: Huchinson.

Osborn, A.F. (1977). *Your Creative Power: How to Use Imagination.* New York: Scribner.

Osborn, A.F. (1979). *Applied Imagination: Principles and Procedures of Creative Problem-Solving.* New York: Scribner.

Von Oech, R. (1983). *A Whack on the Side of the Head: How to Unlock Your Mind for Innovation.* New York: Warner Books.

Young, J.W. (1940). *A Technique for Producing Ideas.* Chicago: Crain Communications.

~ How to Get Better Creative Work ~

1. *Brief in depth, allow time, stay in touch.* Make sure the brief is agreed all the way up the ladder. Mine data for insights. Set realistic deadlines, with time for ideas to incubate. (Agencies are often too optimistic when they commit to due dates, especially under client pressure.) Help ideas survive and thrive. Encourage the agency to aim high. Don't sit back and wait. Show that you are enthusiastic about the project, and keen to see ideas.

2. *Be a leader.* Have a clear vision of where the brand needs to go. Run a tight operation that wants results *and* respects people. Stick your neck out for what you believe in, but don't insist on getting your way every time. Take an agency recommendation up the line, and don't change your mind if the going gets tough. Allow your agency access to management over the occasional stalemate—rather than taking the guts out of a recommendation by compromise.

3. *Involve Agency people in all aspects of your business.* This capitalizes on one of the strengths of an agency—the diversity of its experience. It's more than feeding them the latest data. Keep them abreast of the questions that concern you and the brand. On big issues ask for input from the agency's senior management. If you are interested in the agency's point of view, they will be highly motivated.

4. *Comment on advertising honestly, quickly, objectively; encourage experimentation.* If it's good, praise it. If it isn't, say so. Be positive, but still be honest and direct. Above all, be constructive. Give a sound reason for your view—if you can't, don't make the comment. Beware of personal idiosyncrasies and prejudices. Don't nit-pick or stall ideas that the agency likes but you don't—kill the project or progress it. Resist the temptation to fall back on the familiar. Set up an experimental budget to test controversial advertising. This stimulates creative freedom.

5. *Build a strong personal relationship.* This immeasurably increases the chance of getting superior work. Teamwork (with no reprisal for the occasional failure) works best. Get to know the agency people. Then, if the relationship hits a rough spot, clear and candid communication is that much easier.

6. *Be enthusiastic, challenging, confident, complimentary, and fun to work with.* People work to expectations. And enthusiasm is contagious. This should extend to the feedback you give. Give praise—it's a tonic that balances out criticism. And have some fun.

Do this and the agency will be hungry to produce its very best work for you.

Overview: Chapter Seven

There's a story (I've modified it a bit) that a brain surgeon met a qualitative researcher at a party, and they got talking about what they both did for a living. After a while the brain surgeon said, "That's absolutely fascinating. I think I'd like to do that when I retire." "That's funny," said the researcher, "because when I retire, I'm thinking I would like to be a brain surgeon."

Qualitative research *is* fascinating, but it also needs to be handled with the skill of a brain surgeon.

When we asked Lisa Elder to write this chapter, she had so many potential themes that it was difficult to know where to focus. She settled on *actionability*.

Most of us can relate to projects that start with "let's do some groups" and finish with a report that creates a bit of a stir, flickers briefly on the radar screen, and then falls into oblivion.

There is a better way to do it, as you will see.

Chapter Seven

Quality Action from Qualitative Research

LISA ELDER

Introduction

When I was asked to write this chapter I was happy that qualitative had been given a special role, and was not under the catch-all of research. This is because qualitative, used well, unlocks insights in ways that quantitative simply can't, especially in finding those emotional triggers that are at the core of great brands.

You may have a marketing program that is missing the mark in an indefinable way. Or an advertising campaign that is not shifting the needle. Or a brand with a fleeting grip on the consumer's heart and mind. We've all wrestled with problems like these. Qualitative can ignite a breakthrough in all these areas. But how should it fit in? All too often, the call goes out "Let's do some groups." My hope is that this chapter will give a better approach—one you can put into practice day to day.

The chapter has four sections, each in two parts: current practice (which can be less than ideal), then suggestions for best practice. Examples come from my experience, the public domain, and a special qualitative study I conducted for this exercise—with clients, research managers, creative and account management people, planners, and consultants. Quotes from this punctuate the chapter.

There are very different opinions out there. I will try to show how to harness these often conflicting feelings to the good of the brand.

1 A. Instigating Qualitative Research

There is little debate that, done well and interpreted well, there are many upsides to qualitative. The following word associations were typical:

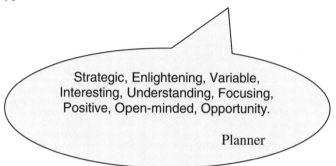

It (re)introduces the consumer to the marketers (across all disciplines).
- It brings depth and texture to flat, factual, horizons of consumer learning.
- It provides insights into specific issues and opportunities.
- It raises comfort levels with decisions, especially when there's a fork in the road (but see a discussion of decision-making later).

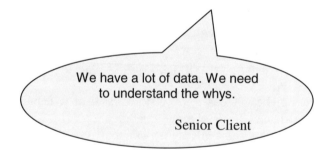

Some are quick to identify why qualitative research has risen in importance in recent years:

- The need to focus on innovation in order to grow.
- The need to breathe life into old brands.
- The focus on building consumer relationships, and therefore the need to understand consumer language and thinking better.

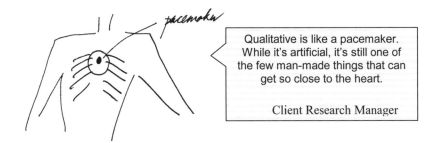

> Qualitative is like a pacemaker. While it's artificial, it's still one of the few man-made things that can get so close to the heart.
>
> Client Research Manager

- Marketers finding themselves far removed from the niche groups that they need for growth (teenaged girls, ethnic markets, etc.).
- Junior marketers seeking direction and clarity under the knee-jerk speed and stress of business today.
- The comparatively painless cost/timing/implementation compared to large-scale quantitative studies.

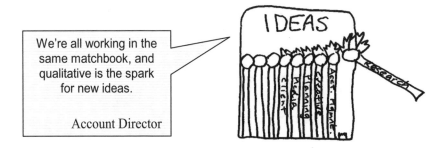

> We're all working in the same matchbook, and qualitative is the spark for new ideas.
>
> Account Director

But there are complaints about why qualitative research is instigated and how.

- Clients procuring qualitative because there isn't time or money to do quantitative—in other words, when the "right problem to be solved" requires statistically significant facts.
- Clients using qualitative learning as if it is quantitatively reliable.
- Any given player seizing on the opinions of a handful of respondents unilaterally, over the collective judgment of the team.
- Qualitative being done "one-off" instead of being part of a considered process.
- Doing it too late.
- Doing it to judge ideas, rather than to inspire them.

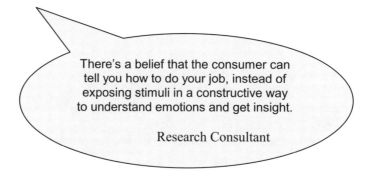

There's a belief that the consumer can tell you how to do your job, instead of exposing stimuli in a constructive way to understand emotions and get insight.

Research Consultant

- Moving too quickly to groups, not touching base with the whole team. (This is a particular issue with creative people, who feel they don't have input to the research but have to live by its results.)
- On the other side of this coin, a feeling from clients that creative, planning, and account management people can be protective and defensive.

There is a love-hate relationship between qualitative research and the agency, particularly the creative people. They love it when qualitative is used very early in the process. When it can acquaint them with how consumers *think and feel*, on top of what they do and buy. When it sheds light on core behaviour and beliefs. When it clarifies how a brand fits into consumers' lives, and quite possibly why.

They hate it—with good reason—when qualitative is used to judge and measure instead of inform and inspire. When consumers are brought in to evaluate creative *output* when the time or money wasn't spent getting consumer *input* before the ideas were created. When an influential client attends one focus group, takes the comments as gospel … and trashes an idea. When clients believe that research participants are the be-all and end-all, instead (assuming valid recruiting) of being just a helpful element in the marketing process. When they are told, often wearily, that "research shows" participants can envision the future from a cartoon drawing of a script, and react to it emotionally, when no one else on the team can.

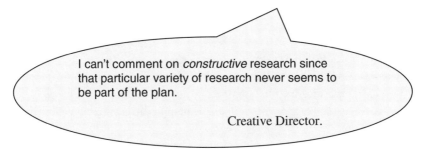

I can't comment on *constructive* research since that particular variety of research never seems to be part of the plan.

Creative Director.

This conflict between those who commission research and those who have to use it can make the whole exercise of qualitative research debilitating instead of liberating. It is a major issue, but it can be solved, as we shall see.

1 B. Best Practices for Instigating Qualitative

a) Use Qualitative to Build, Not Kill.

The smart way to use qualitative is to build and refine, instead of measure and judge. This does not preclude pithy, actionable results. But you get more than just go/no-go answers. You get context, perspectives, and stories—things that any team member can draw upon for a considerable time, well beyond the strategic or tactical decisions of the day.

Here are three mindsets that will predict if your qualitative will likely kill or build:

Qualitative that Kills		Qualitative that Builds
Have something to test	→	Have something to discover
Done as an afterthought		Done with forethought
Want the right answer		Want knowledge for an inspired solution

Qualitative gets used in the wrong way for reasons we discussed earlier. More important, though, is what can be done to improve matters. It is crucial for *decision-makers* (usually in client marketing and research) to refuse to do what ultimately will not be right for the brand. As David Ogilvy wrote:

> I admit that research is often misused by agencies and clients. They have a way of using it to prove they are right. They use research as a drunkard uses a lamppost—not for illumination but for support. On the whole, however, research can be of incalculable help in producing more effective advertising.[1]

b) *Think in Terms of Pre-search,*™ *Not Research.*[2]

I love the meaning of re-search—to search again for inspiring answers that others might have missed. With that in mind, turn the typical process on its head. Rather than doing research after the fact (all too frequent nowadays), start everything earlier. Treat every phase as a fresh look at the brand. For instance, instead of only testing creative, explore alternative communication strategies. But before dwelling on these, determine the hows and whys of your strongest brand strategy. Before that, ask yourself if you know enough about the meaning and texture of consumer and category behaviour.

---

1 To see research used in the way Lisa is describing, see the "Got Milk" campaign, in *Truth. Lies & Advertising* by Jon Steel.

2 As business pressure has increased, so has the tendency to do research reactively. Lisa coined Presearch.™ as a process of thinking about research in an "upstream" way.

Throughout it all, look for consumer insights.

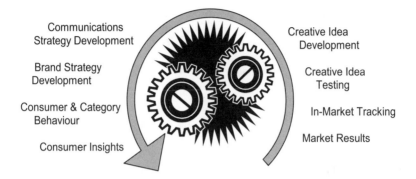

Communications Strategy Development

Brand Strategy Development

Consumer & Category Behaviour

Consumer Insights

Creative Idea Development

Creative Idea Testing

In-Market Tracking

Market Results

The counter-clockwise arrow is a reminder to roll back the role of qualitative from evaluation (too little, too late) to learning and ideas. This brings the whole team together with deeper understanding and better judgments—rather than being at odds over the research.

I have been asked point blank if creative people would ever embrace qualitative research. If used in the way I am describing, the answer is a resounding yes.

c) Create a Research Plan, rather than Ad-hoc Research Projects.

One of the best planning models is a simple series of five questions:[3]

- Where is the brand now?
- Why is it here?
- Where could it be?
- How can we get it there?
- Are we getting there?

These questions are always hovering over the brand, and there are big opportunities for integrating the answers into the marketing planning cycle.

---

3 See the footnote regarding these questions in Andy Macaulay's chapter.

Qualitative can be a shaky foundation after the fact, but it can be very strong when it is part of the input. Integrate the insights early, since you can't change the flower after it's bloomed.

Account Director

The cry for "Let's do some groups!" will be replaced by a plan to find the touch-points that really move consumers. Hold a team meeting, early. Agree what you know about your brand and consumer, and what you don't. From this, identify which research effort will most impact the brand. Have a top researcher at this meeting, to give you ideas and methodologies—and remember the value of starting sooner.

d) Craft a Thoughtful Research Brief, with Input from the Team.

Considering the cost and impact of qualitative, it's a wonder that research briefs are a rarity. This compounds the problem for the team. They don't have a forum to input to the objectives—and ultimately have little say in what research is conducted. In contrast, a well-crafted brief, supported by a thoughtful Consumer Research Plan, prompts better research design, and results the team can act on with confidence and enthusiasm. It also gives the researcher the chance to think out of the box, and to present more-than-the-obvious in terms of techniques and approaches.

What the Researcher Typically Needs to Know

Objectives:
What is the product or service you're doing research for?
What is the problem or opportunity?
What are the most important questions you're seeking answers for?
Why will the answers make a difference?
What actions will be taken as a result of the research?

Target:
Who are the target purchasers?
Who are you most interested in involving in the research? (Please prioritize)
Do you have beliefs about these people, and how sure are you about these beliefs?

Methodology:
Is there a particular type of research you're thinking of? If so, describe what and why.

History:
Has research been done in this area? Please list/provide all information available.

Geography:
Is the research required nationally or is it specific to particular markets or regions? (Note their relative importance.)

Competition:
Are there particular things about the competition that need to be taken into account?

Budget:
What is the research budget?

Process/Timing:
When is the research proposal required? Desired in-field date (noting any better or worse times, seasonality factors).
What is the approval process for this project?
Team Members (names and roles).
Key contact, others.

Background:
Attach information that will be beneficial to this research (i.e. historical research, brand strategy, creative strategy, target information, media plan, competitive information.)

2 A. Designing Qualitative

Some qualitative is best explored by techniques like one-on-one interviews or ethnographic research. In their best light, focus groups are based on regular folk who represent the audience/issue in question. They are made comfortable, and expertly encouraged to express their thoughts—including those that are below the surface. The facility will be well equipped (or otherwise appropriate). Marketers/agencies etc. will be able to listen and observe, and have a say in what is probed.

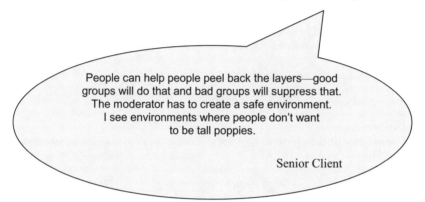

In their worst light, groups are too contrived. Respondents attend so many groups that they approach questions "professionally" instead of instinctively. They are in an uninspiring setting that's disconnected from their lives and their brand(s)—and their comments can't even be heard by those who are gossiping in the back room.

This dichotomy came through very clearly in word associations of the good and the bad in qualtitative research. We saw the positive associations earlier. The negative ones came out like a poignant free-form short poem:

Frustrating, Vapid, Bang my head against the wall,
Suffocate, Waste of time,
Hollow man,
Repetition,
Will there be food?

There are many other forums to consider, beyond focus groups:

Mini-groups:
- Groups of 4 respondents to increase intimacy and discussion.
- Preferred if there are lots of materials, if you want to encourage free discussion and perhaps also a bit of controversy.
- Think of women's life stages, how breastfeeding Moms feel about formula, how teachers feel about new financial products.

Paired interviews:
- Two consumers with one researcher, can be strangers or friends.
- Limits groupthink.
- Much better than groups for exploring/evaluating creative approaches.
- Think of how 8 to 10-year-old girls respond to new retail advertising, how girlfriends feel about tea, how seniors versus young professionals feel about door-to-door selling tactics.

In-depth individual interviews (IDIs):
- One consumer with one researcher.
- Great for personal perspectives, devoid of group interaction.
- Especially suitable for very personal topics. Also useful when there is a lot of competition between people.
- Think of obese women and diet pills, surgeons and pharmaceutical companies, men trying to quit smoking, teens with acne.

2 B. Best Practices for Qualitative Design

a) Use Untapped Techniques to Discover Untapped Opportunities.

Ingenuity in how and when you approach consumers will show your brand and products in a new and inspiring light.

b) Use Variety to Capture What Consumers Experience.

Add texture to focus groups with cross-country Internet groups, and half a dozen ethnographic interviews. Merge focus groups with more experiential and personal techniques, even without "witnesses," to add insights and meaning.

c) Give the Researcher Room to Breathe.

One of the skills of a moderator is *listening*, and to do this the Discussion Guide must have some space in it. If you work with guides, make sure they contain only what is essential. If there is nitty-gritty you want to find out, consider gleaning the answers through "homework," or by asking respondents to do an exercise in the lobby while they're waiting for research to begin.

d) Consider the Following Possibilities.

Observational research:

- Watch what your target does, sometimes with them unaware.
- Imagine teens shopping for videos, men reading the newspaper, children using coffee shops.

Experiential research:

- Work with consumers to understand how they experience a product/service.
- Move along with the consumers as they do their thing.
- Imagine Christmas shopping with Moms for kids under ten, eating tacos for dinner with families of teens, seeing how vets approach business accounting.

Ethnographic research:

- Combine observational, experiential, one-on-one (or family) conversations.
- Typically done for 3 or more hours per respondent.
- Done by an ethnography expert, and hands-off, initially, by the researcher.
- An outstanding approach for understanding deep-rooted human behaviour.
- Imagine a study on breakfast, revealing what a megabrand taps into—that its competitor does not and cannot.

e) Look at Ways of Changing how Qualitative is Done.

Online focus groups:

- Link up target consumers for a chat online.
- Get written responses to questions posed by a moderator.
- Review online graphic materials and witness web-browsing.
- Send secret responses to participants, or to the moderator.
- Great for reaching geographically diverse audiences.
- Think of ad research among farmers cross-Canada, or among charitable contributors from smaller towns, or small business owners.

Online IDIs:

- Create an in-depth one-on-one exchange between consumer and interviewer.
- Issue web-cams for nominal cost and have face-to-face interaction.
- Have "show and tell" and great story telling.
- Think of 11 to 14-year-olds and their most exciting toy ideas, or patients speaking about hospital clinic experiences.

Online bulletin boards:

- Post a series of questions to the target, over the web.
- Distribute questions over a 1 to 5 day time frame.
- Design it to gather their input when the product or service has just been used.
- Think of consumers logging their feelings about pain and pain relievers over a period of days, workers talking about a company training program, what happens every time Mom serves a new food product to her family.

f) Use "Homework" with Participants.

Still pictures:

- Useful for products/services where it's hard to be there at the right time (e.g. adults snacking, or reading, or balancing their finances).
- Will become even easier with the increasing penetration of digital cameras.

Video takes:

- Wonderful for expressing the moment and inspiring ideas.
- Think of kids reporting on the clothes their friends are wearing, and what's hot and what's not.

Collages:

- Built by consumers, using images, music, textures and colours to symbolize and express how they feel.
- Imagine a 3-D collage of all of the roles a woman plays in her life (with a personal goal sticking out of the pyramid!), or a collage of all the things a 13-year-old wants for back to school and where he's going to get them.

All of these ways of shifting the goalposts have a staggering ability to produce outstanding insights.

3 A. Conducting Qualitative Research

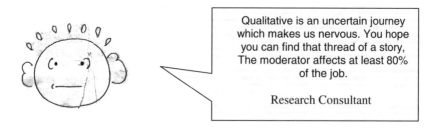

Qualitative is an uncertain journey which makes us nervous. You hope you can find that thread of a story, The moderator affects at least 80% of the job.

Research Consultant

First off, selecting the best moderator is essential. The best-laid plans will fail without a proper conduit to consumers.

Secondly, you must select the best participants. They must be the right target audience for the task at hand, but this is not as guaranteed as it sounds. Facing recruiting difficulties, a recruiting house may "stretch" the definitions too far. Make sure this does not happen to you. Over and above this, there is a debate about the *type* of participant. There is a real problem of focus group junkies—who make the rounds of groups, sometimes with axes to grind, sometimes loving to perform, sometimes just there for the food and the nice envelope.

> Brand managers don't know about recruiting from files… it's the trailer park folks coming out and doing their thing.
>
> Research Consultant

Recruiters and moderators must be vigilant. The Professional Market Research Society (PMRS) has been trying to raise the quality of recruits. As recently as last year they mandated that research facilities require that ID match the prerecruited lists. Another solution, though difficult, is to invite only first timers.

Alternatively, you might want participants who are extra articulate. Given that qualitative is (ideally) for ideas, inspiration, watch-outs and opportunities, why not find the thought-leaders? If they are virginal participants, so much the better.

> I want it to be a group of aspirational people, better able to talk and articulate, versus being too mainstream and ordinary.
>
> Account Director

As already noted, you need to select or create the best environment. Often, the most natural setting is ideal:

- By the corner shop to talk to teens about snack foods
- In a guy's basement with his friends to review programming
- At a model home to consider reactions to smart wiring systems
- Right at the store, once they've had a chance to shop around

This is where focus group facilities fall very short, and other arenas can be more stimulating.

3 B. Best Practices for Conducting Qualitative Research

a) Choose the Right Person for the Job, Beyond Just the Company.

Some questions as you search for a qualitative partner:

- How do they view brands? Do their philosophies concur with yours? Will they stretch your knowledge into new areas of opportunity?
- Do they show an interest and aptitude for your project beyond the necessities? Do they have an insightful mind and a strong sense of directed curiosity? Do their questions lead you to new ideas, even in the planning stages?
- Are they imaginative and creative? Look for it in their work, their suggested methods, their ways of exploring your problem.
- Do they have a talent for conducting groups *and* turning the results into recommendations you can use? Do they have a gift for identifying *meaning* from findings? Are they passionate about solutions, while not prejudging what those solutions might be?
- Are they highly recommended by those you know and respect?

b) Select the Right Respondents.

Do you want the great unwashed? Do you want super consumers? Do you want friends, or family members? Do you want people by demographic profile or by attitude or behaviour? Even better, what combination of techniques and respondents will create a new buzz of learning?

c) *Select the Right Environment.*

Don't go where it's convenient, go where your target group gathers—where they buy a brand, or use it, or evaluate it (or all three). Break out of old patterns. Put the team on the front line, not in a back room. I've had a lot of success putting one or two amenable creative people in the same room as consumers—thinking, drawing, asking questions. (This gives them a feel for consumers firsthand, and is great for team-building.)

d) *Keep People in the Back Room Stimulated.*

I know it's fun, but we have to stop taking potshots at the third lady on the right. Give the "viewers" a Hot Thought Sheet, looking for the most quotable, most surprising, most inspiring, most actionable. These sheets can be a goldmine for the moderator during debriefing.

Get the team into the field with the researcher—let them see the consumer eat the product, use the service, surf the net, install the equipment, shop the store, call the company. Work as a team, afterwards, to distill the experiences into action.

4 A. Incorporating Qualitative Learning

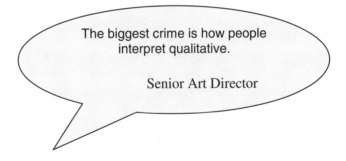

The biggest crime is how people interpret qualitative.

Senior Art Director

There are far fewer issues with how qualitative is conducted, and far more with how the learning is interpreted. The most damaging behaviours:

- *Selective Perception:* Having what one consumer says stick irrevocably in your head—instead of listening for, and identifying, common themes that always emerge over the course of a study.
- *The Drop-In Syndrome:* Basing your POV only on the consumers you heard (sometimes less than one full session) rather than on the experience collected across the entire project.
- *False Validity:* Treating the learning as statistically projectible, rather than as an aid to judgment. There is a reason for that "non-projectibility" disclaimer.

4 B. Best Practices for Incorporating Qualitative Learning

a) *Encourage Outcomes That Inspire, Not Just Inform.*

With the right moderator this will be one of their primary objectives—but make it an objective for all team members:

- To search, not destroy.
- To have the whole team (including creative) in the planning meeting.
- To include the full team in the research itself.
- To keep the back room positive and focused on the task.

b) *Close the Timing Gap Between the Research and the Reporting.*

As a moderator, I ask for time to deliver a well thought out point of view, but from my agency days I know that rush-to-judgment interpretations can take hold while this is being done. Head this off by working with the moderator to get the fastest possible, effective, debrief.

c) *Use Moderated Debriefs.*

With the classic debrief (where moderators give their opinion, often to the malevolent silence of some of the team) the *essence* of qualitative is lost. It is a stimulus for finding great new ways to build the brand, and what better way to get this than to make the debrief a discussion, not a lecture.

Conclusion

The value of understanding consumers is second to none. Qualitative research—done with forethought, imagination and integrity—is unbeatable in its ability to inspire new directions and ideas. And the results aren't just interesting, they can have a profound effect on the future of a brand.

Knowing you have good results:	Knowing they are actionable:
You have new perspectives and texture versus before.	The team has a new (or confirmed) vision for marketing the brand.
You've extracted knowledge and insight from information.	The team has turned this into inspiration.

Marshall McLuhan said, "When all is said and done, more will have been said than done." I hope these few pages tip the balance towards getting more done.

Overview: Chapter Eight

We had an issue with this chapter. How to handle the disagreements that swirl around advertising research.

There is the well-known antipathy of creative people. There are less public (but still entrenched) disputes in the research community. There are clients who more or less agree with what might be called the "general client approach." But there are others, including some marquee names, who are diametrically opposed to it.

We were not sure who could best speak on the subject. Whoever we asked might be seen as a representative of one stance or another.

As we cast around for a victim, my name came up.

Research is not my field, but I've spent my whole career close to it. I'm also not attached to a school of thought, except the belief that research is wonderful when used well and interpreted thoughtfully, and seductively dangerous otherwise.

So I was asked to jump into the tiger pit.

Chapter Eight

Advertising and Research—Why Such Uneasy Bedfellows?

DAVID RUTHERFORD

Introduction

So much has been said. Legendary names have argued one view or another. Papers have espoused different and often contradictory ideas. Anecdotal evidence has been hailed or reviled, with selective perception that would make an axe-grinder blush. And everyday projects throw client, agency, and research people together—usually under the mantle of civility, but often with loggerheads lurking beneath the surface.

For reasons we'll come to, I think that a lot of this tension is inevitable, though not (if handled constructively) always a bad thing.

In any event, I'm not going to try to wrestle the conflicting views into submission. I have a more dispassionate objective: to cover the subject in an even-handed way, in the hope that this will help people come to better decisions—about research in general, but more particularly about brands.

This means that this is not a chapter about techniques (except by inference), but it is a "how to" chapter in the broad sense.

The Analogy of Comparative Religion

If you talk to a zealot about religion you don't get very far. Even *the existence of other views* is intolerable. With advertising research it gets interesting:

- Most creative people are anti-research-as-it-is-practised-today.[1] Most are zealots (some vociferous) and make no apology for it.
- Researchers don't see themselves as zealots—having a self-concept closer to "purveyors of objective reality." From my experience, though, many are zealots deep down. They conduct themselves as if they, uniquely, have the keys to revealed truth.[2]
- Most clients want simple (and inexpensive) answers to complex questions. We often do what is pragmatic over what is right.
- Given all this, it's not surprising that there's tension.

Where the Bedfellows Agree, at Least Up to a Point

The basic steps to brand-building are pretty much agreed:

1. Decide how to position the brand to make it the most appealing choice, now, and over the long term.
2. Decide the best way for the brand to tell its story.[3]
3. Produce execution(s), making sure they deliver what was intended.
4. Measure in-market results.
5. Apply the lessons to future activity.

Within this, however, there are big differences of opinion. At Steps 1 and 2 above, creative people usually want more research, especially qualitative. Step 4 can lead to debate about "are we measuring the right thing in the right way" and (like Steps 1 and 2) can lead to disputes over interpretation. But the main friction comes at Step 3.

---

1 The antipathy is mostly against quantitative pre-testing, as we shall see.
2 Such researchers act as if their body of knowledge is holy writ. They don't reveal that behind the scenes academics and researchers are lobbing intellectual hand-grenades at each other, furiously challenging opposing schools of thought.
3 There is a lot in these eleven words, of course, as covered in other chapters.

From the creative point of view, the prevailing attitude is like this:

Upfront Qualitative	Quantitative Pretesting	In-Market Tracking
Usually want more of it.	Hate it.	Agree that it makes sense.

The Bone of Contention

Paul Feldwick was Convenor of Judges for the 1998 and 2000 IPA Effectiveness Awards. He is a top planner in the UK, and is passionate about accountability. In "A brief guided tour through the copy-testing jungle" (*Admap*, 1998) he reviews the stances to creative pretesting, and sets up the following spectrum of attitudes:

Paul Feldwick's Spectrum of Attitudes to Creative Pretesting

Unaided judgment	Judgment aided by research	Research interpreted by judgment	Research (quantitative) as predictor
No predictive research	Usually qualitative	Usually quantitative	Little use of judgment

Disagreement flares when one side faces off against another. As noted, those on the left of the spectrum are often zealots, but so are those on the right. Referring to them, Feldwick's paper starts like this:

> Quantitative testing embraces a number of quite radically different techniques, based on different theories and assumptions about how advertising works. It is also a highly competitive marketplace, where the suppliers of each technique will tend to stress the merits of their particular method with a bewildering degree of conviction.[4]

---

4 Bewildering because no one has a monopoly on the answers.

Why the Spectrum?

In his chapter, Rupert Brendon talks about two world views. They explain this spectrum:

The "Creative" View	The "Business" View
The best way to reach people is to touch them in ways they have never been touched before. That's what I do.	We all know why we're here. Advertising is a tool to do a job. I want the best, most effective, tool for doing that job.

The creative view is not exclusive to agencies, of course. The clients behind some great brands (e.g. Nike, Levi's, Absolut Vodka) reject the "business" view as mechanistic. Like creative people, they feel that quantitative pretesting *kills or damages* the chance of getting the best creative for building brands.

Those who favour quantitative pretesting don't accept this stance, and many are suspicious of it. Like the advocates of lie detectors, they pointedly wonder why creative people are unwilling to have their work put to the test. So, the ancient (and in my view misguided) feud between creativity and effectiveness lives on.

Should the Feud Exist?

Before I was herded into the bullpen at P&G I was a Civil Engineer. Civil Engineers are cousins to quantitative researchers.[5] Architects, the good ones, are kin to creative people. Dyed-in-the-wool engineers would say, "Those mince pies can come up with buildings that look pretty, but you can't build them." I'm not sure if architects thought much about engineers, except possibly wondering if they should tip us.

The Sydney Opera House was a lightning rod for this sniping. When first proposed, the engineers said it couldn't be built. And construction was a nightmare. But eventually it was finished, and now it's one of the great buildings in the world.

---

5 This comment may or may not apply to me. After 21 months as a Civil Engineer I was fired.

Tension between the great (though potentially risky or impractical) and the tried-and-true (though likely pedestrian) seems to be inescapable. But should it be?

One of the problems in advertising is the way the debate is framed. Those on the left of our spectrum see pretesting as the evil eye. Those on the right seem to think creativity is joined at the hip to irrelevance and self-indulgence.

Is there justification for these stereotypes? Unfortunately yes. Some pretesting is brutish and insensitive. Some creativity is glaringly irresponsible. But why do we allow that to obscure something more important. Nike, Levi's and Absolut Vodka, amongst others, see "creativity" and "tool to do a job" as two sides of the coin. Several examples in the Cassies reflect the same point.

One of the agencies has captured the goal in an ingenious turn of phrase: *Surprise that makes Sense.* This is surely better than feuding.

Is the Tension Inevitable—and Does It Have to Be a Bad Thing?

In her chapter, Lisa Elder argues that it's possible, and wonderful for the brand, to bring "creative" and "research" views together. I agree, but Lisa is talking about qualitative research. When it comes to quantitative pretesting, the lines are drawn more deeply in the sand. Disagreements are often not handled gracefully.

Voltaire famously said, "I disagree with what you say, but will fight to the death for your right to say it." This would be an excessive sacrifice for a piece of creative, but we know what he meant.

I was once part of a particularly disputatious client-agency-research triangle, and the client said, "Can't we all just get along?" The question was understandable. But is unanimity, achieved by compromise, a good thing? It isn't necessarily so.

Client

Agency   Research

Business has been struggling for a 100 years or more to predict if advertisements are going to work. If anyone had found the answer (*really* found the answer) the struggle would be over. Yes, there is a substantial pretesting business, but not on a scale that says that someone has found the Holy Grail. Dear old homo sapiens refuses to be predictable when it comes to advertising, despite the "bewildering degree of conviction" that comes not only from researchers, but also others who make up the triangle.

Disagreement is inevitable. But how should we handle it? Compromise seems to be the worst option. Throughout history, great ideas have been inspired by magnificent clashes. Clients especially should not be knocked off-stride by differences between agencies and researchers. Let them fight for what they believe. Insist that they take Voltaire's highroad, but don't worry if the sparks fly—this can make the ultimate decision better.

Is Everybody Comfortable?

I've seen creative approved under all sorts of circumstances. A partial list:

- By a benevolent dictator, overriding the misgivings of others, sometimes listening to research, and sometimes not.[6]
- After an almost unanimous "that's it!" (with no research).
- Pumped by the idea, "If I feel nervous, that has to be good."[7]
- Driven by research yardsticks, with creative people feeling their ideas have been shredded in the process.
- As a result of a charismatic creative team, with researchers feeling their advice has been ignored.
- With clients feeling under pressure to get something out there, but unsure that the creative is right.
- With clients so determined to do something out of the box that they throw caution to the winds.

If any of these approaches had a conspicuously better batting average than the others, I probably wouldn't be writing this chapter. But to varying degrees they have all had their successes and failures. The successes get celebrated, sometimes disproportionately, and the failures go quietly to unmarked graves. This makes it impossible to assess all this objectively.

---

6 This has been true for many famous campaigns, that might otherwise have died in a cross-fire of concerns.

7 Some risks should be taken, but it's not very bright to go swimming with crocodiles. See the "right risk" in Chapter 6.

What I don't understand, though, is the question, "Is everybody comfortable?" Breakthrough ideas don't strike everyone the same way. Some people will be exhilarated. Some will be distinctly *un*-comfortable. I'd like to suggest we consign this question to its own spot in the cemetery of bad practice.

Different Mental Models

Differences over research are often a sign of deeper-rooted disagreements. I'd like to explore this, with the forewarning that it does not converge to a single neat answer.

To start, we have to accept that there is no universal theory to explain why, when, how, or if advertising works. Theories that explain everything are so broad as to be useless. Specific ones fail to account for the exceptions that immediately come to mind.

This shouldn't be a surprise. For anything to do with how we "think, feel, and do" there is no theory to explain it all. Religion, psychiatry, the social sciences—even the hard sciences—have multiple camps and tribal demarcations. Einstein came up with the Theory of Relativity as a comparatively young man, and spent the rest of his life trying to find what has since been called the "Theory of Everything." Some academics have set a similar goal for advertising, but we are still waiting.

H.L. Mencken (a singularly unpleasant man, but a brilliant social critic) said:

> At the heart of every complex problem is a simple answer—which is wrong.

This is too tough to handle in our line of work, because *business hates complexity and uncertainty.* We need that simple answer. So we develop mental models. Whether we realize it or not, these are "works for me" ideas that don't account for the complexity (and contradiction) that advertising entails. Let's look at some of the knottier issues.

a) The Question of Basic Economic Sense

There is ultimately only one reason for a client to invest in advertising. To get, as Fagin said in *Oliver*, in the bank large amounts—more than would accrue by doing something else with the money.

One of the ironies of advertising is that those not making decisions about it (many economists, consumerists and social scientists) see it as an all-powerful capitalist tool, bending the mindless masses to its will. It does not occur to them that if this were true, advertising expenditures would have exploded exponentially, and this certainly has not happened. As insiders, we know that when advertising has to prove that it makes economic sense—not in general, but in the current fiscal, with those red-blooded volume and profit targets, and multiple other demands on the budget—the going gets decidedly heavy. Here's what is known about this:

- Advertising (when the creative is right) has a short *and* a long-term effect.[8]
- The short-term effect, on occasion, is sufficient to justify itself in immediate terms (e.g. in a twelve-month period), as shown by many Cassies winners, and the IPA Effectiveness Awards in the UK.[9]
- However, quite often, the short-term effect is not enough to pay for itself immediately. This opens up the question, "If we stopped advertising, would we lose business." In many categories it has been shown experimentally (and by experience) that the business does *not* drop like a stone.
- This last point puts advertising budgets under pressure, especially from those (e.g. finance directors) who do not have, or do not want to have, an understanding of the short and long-term picture.
- The long-term *damage* of not advertising (shown by various studies and experience) is usually a logarithmic decay. A brand can coast on momentum for a year or so, declining quite gently, before it runs into real trouble. The irony is agonizing. A brand can become strong with the help of advertising, but this very fact makes it vulnerable to those who want to dis-invest.
- The long-term *benefit* of advertising (when the creative is right) has been demonstrated repeatedly by companies like P&G.

---

8 When the creative is "wrong" advertising does not make economic sense. We know this from experience. In addition, studies with split-cable test markets show that media weight alone is not enough to build business economically. It is not enough just to get the name out. The creative has to be effective.

9 The Effies also deserve mention, though they demand somewhat less rigorous proof.

- It has also been demonstrated in IRI's split-cable Behaviourscan markets in the US. These allow marketers to test different approaches (creative and media weight mainly) and see the effect on the business. As a result of "an unprecedented US industry collaboration" authors Lodish and Lubetkin were able to examine the results. On the question of long-term effects, they say the following:

  > It has long been hypothesized that advertising can have a significant long-term impact on sales. However that has not in the past been supported by any empirical data. Today, we have the data that lays that issue to rest.

  They take markets that achieved a 22% sales increase in Year I versus control because of ad activity. They then describe the "carryover effect" on the next two years (from this point on, the test and control areas got the same plan). They found that the growth in Years II and III, when added together, was another 21%. In other words, the growth across three years was virtually double the growth in the first year, with no incremental spending. This type of finding is also validated by impeccable sources such as the PIMS database.[10]
- The major research houses (though they have different views about how advertising works) have various "longitudinal" studies that show a long-tem advertising effect. As already noted, of course, this is not indiscriminately true—the creative has to be effective.
- There are different views as to how the long-term benefit builds up. One is that the long-term is merely an accumulation of the short-term—i.e. if you get short-term growth, and keep it coming, you finish up with long-term growth. Another (dare I say more complex) view is that we retrieve advertising impressions, consciously or unconsciously, at the propitious moment. This may be now, or it may be some time into the future.

---

10 The PIMS database (Profit Impact of Marketing Strategy) originated at General Electric, then transferred to Harvard for a while, and has since been perpetuated by the Strategic Planning Institute as a huge, rigorous databank "designed to measure the relationship between business actions and business results." Note that although it throws light on advertising activity it has no connection to the advertising industry.

- Related to this, there are different ideas about whether a business should focus on attracting new users, or keeping *current* ones. Attracting new users is often expensive (6 x more is often quoted) than keeping current users. Brands will usually have to do both, but the distinction is important, because advertising to achieve these two goals might have to be very different.
- In the client-agency-research triangle there can be very different mental models for all this. They are often not articulated—and many disagreements trace back to this.

b) *The Role of the Advertising*

In the show "Bewitched" a client (let's say a shoe manufacturer) comes to Larry Tate and says, "I need an ad campaign to sell my shoes." Larry says, "You've come to the right place" and hands the job to Darrin Stevens. Darrin comes up with the idea, and (with the help of a bit of magic) sells the idea to the client. It works, and everyone is happy.

No one asks, "what is the *essence* of the shoe-wearing experience?" There's no SWOT analysis to assess the competitive frame of reference. No one says, "What is the role of the advertising?" They just get on with it.

Echoes of this still exist. Some people see the effort that goes into strategy development, then idea development, then the evaluation of those ideas, and a small voice wonders, "does it really take all this to sell a pair of shoes?"

As a matter of fact, talented people can, on occasion, come up with a brilliantly effective campaign in a magically short period of time. But it usually takes more than this. The reasons are worth restating:

- Consumers have many brands to choose from.
- Products are often very similar.
- Consumers are bombarded with promotional effort.
- When they pay attention, they are increasingly sophisticated in sorting out what rings true and what doesn't.

In this world, "I just want to sell more shoes" isn't enough. Should advertising glorify the shoes? With what message—functional, emotional, or both? Is the objective to get people to the store? (as with a lot of car advertising). Is it to attract new users, or current users? Are we trying to enhance what people already think, or change their minds? As with Nike, is it about the shoes at all, or about tapping into a state of mind? Or, as with the "Manhattan" campaign for British Airways, is the real objective to influence the stock market?

These questions force difficult choices. When I was first in brand management I asked the agency, "Why can't we do them all?" Those who didn't roll their eyes forced a patient smile. Hard choices have to be made—something that P&G called "the pain of leaving things out."

This is why it is so crucial to pin down the role of advertising. When there are too many objectives (and this seems to happen a lot) research will not necessarily measure the right thing. Conflict is then inevitable.

c) Preconceptions

I'll illustrate this with the story of concentrated "all." It was an excellent Lever product, developed for front-loading washing machines. It was quite expensive, and a low-sudser (something only a minority of consumers wanted). Front-loaders did not catch on, and in English Canada "all" was one tenth the size of Tide.

Then, Lever added a new perfume, and supported it with syrupy soft-sell advertising. Mommy and Daddy read bedtime stories to kids in fluffy PJs; a little girl in a birthday dress asks Daddy if she looks pretty—that sort of thing. I was Brand Manager on Tide, and we thought Lever had gone mad. But over the next two years "all" doubled its share because of this advertising. We asked ourselves, "what do they know that we don't know?"

Then the twist. I left P&G, and, after a year of purification in the wilderness, joined O&M. My first brand was "all." Imagine my astonishment when I was told that Lever's senior management hated the campaign. We had to get "all" back to hard-sell heaven. We resisted, but got a read-my-lips directive. We did the best we could, but nothing worked. The nail in the coffin came a few years later when Lever, to save money, de-concentrated the product and raised the sudsing level, thus removing the last vestige of any point of difference.

Another preconception, this time one of mine, was equally off-base. I saw the "Get Cracking" campaign turn egg consumption around by making eggs "healthy, active and vigorous." Campbell's Soup was in the doldrums, and I thought we should make it "healthy active and vigorous" too. We produced a campaign called "Get that Campbell Zip." It passed successfully through Campbell research. But it failed utterly in the marketplace. In those days there was time to learn from your mistakes. Campbell's hired an in-depth researcher called Peter Hume. He confirmed that yes, the Zip campaign communicated what it was supposed to. But he asked people the question that our research had not. Did the advertising ring true? He got a resounding "no." Peter explained it as politely as he could. We had tried to make soup FAST when it is fundamentally SLOW.[11]

The preconceptions in these stories happen to come from client and agency, but researchers are just as prone to them. Some preconceptions turn out to be right, of course. But when disagreement flares, recognize them for what they are, and discuss them candidly, with the blinkers off.

d) Rules of Thumb

Over the years, there have been many attempts to deconstruct advertising into the do's and don'ts of success. Many have found their way into mental models on such topics as:

- When and how often the brand name should appear.
- Whether or not the product needs to be seen in use.
- How the audio and video should interact.
- How much to focus on the solution versus the problem—and so on.

The problem is that if you look at proven work, such as the Cassies and the IPA Awards, you see so many exceptions that these "rules" really should be put out to pasture.[12]

---

11 We then went on to make some very successful advertising. Andy Macaulay uses this story to draw some lessons about strategy development in Chapter 3.

12 For example, some believe that the brand name should come "early and often." But the Cassies winners show a great many exceptions to this. This rule of thumb comes from the Day-after-Recall era, when consumers were not ad-saturated. It strikes me that many audiences today need to be coaxed into a receptive mood before we introduce the brand and make the sale.

Rules of thumb cut both ways of course. Those above are restrictive. The following are designed to liberate:

- Zig when others zag.
- There are no rules but this one.
- Principles endure. Formulas don't. (Bernbach)

Sad to say, there is a tendency to overstate the "evidence" that supports a preconceived view. The major quantitative houses have charts that show a correlation between their techniques and marketplace results—but given how difficult it is to isolate the pure effect of advertising, it's hard to see how this justifies the "bewildering degree of conviction" Paul Feldwick refers to.

On the other side of the coin, those who decry research have been known to use it selectively to suit their purpose. This happened with "liking." To everyone's surprise, the ARF Copy Validity Project in 1991[13] found that "liking" predicted a commercial's in-market success more so than some of the expected factors. This was big news, but what does "liking" mean? Most published work suggests that although it includes "entertaining" it leans more towards "relevant, useful and interesting." Ignoring this, many people seized on the finding and tried to make "must be entertaining" a rule of thumb.[14]

As I said when this section started, the issues don't converge to a neat answer. But, despite what Mencken said, we need *something* that allows us to do our jobs. Let's look at four main streams of thought to see if this helps.

---

13 The study was designed to the highest standards, to examine the predictive ability of pre-testing techniques. It was based on five pairs of commercials, one pair for each of five brands. They had run in split-cable test-markets, with one commercial of each pair being more effective, in-market, than the other. The commercials were rotated through a battery of techniques. The study found a reasonable predictive ability for pretesting in general, but not to the degree that some of the interested parties might have hoped. There followed a storm of claim and counter-claim about the validity of the results.

14 Note: I am not attacking "entertaining" itself. A lot of successful advertising is entertaining. I am attacking the tendency to overstate evidence.

Four Main Streams of Thought

There are countless theories of how advertising works—one of the top UK researchers has identified something like five hundred in the literature. This section is not about that. We are still looking at the tensions that swirl around pretesting. I'll start by summarizing the "no pretesting" view. Then we'll look at the "persuasion" and "recall/awareness" debate. We'll close with comments on approaches that are related to these two, but don't seem to fall into either camp.

For added certainty, as the lawyer's say, this section is not about upfront research for unearthing "truths." Nor is it about ongoing research such as tracking.

a) The "No Pretest" School

This embraces many creative people, and some high-profile clients. In the sense of "no quantitative" it also includes quite a few planners and account people—though they don't always reveal their point of view to unreceptive clients. Some of this group are also against *qualitative pretesting* for go/no-go decisions. The reasons mostly cluster around how the research is interpreted, and how the results are used. Lisa Elder discusses this in her chapter.

To the quantitative camp, the "no pretest" view is beyond the pale. For many it confirms their worst stereotypes. But Janet Kestin and Nancy Vonk (Creative Heads at Ogilvy & Mather), have an unassailable commitment to delivering results. They argued "no pretest" in a recent speech. Key points included:

- We place too much faith in numbers. As the economist Robert Chambers says in *The Tyranny of Numbers,* "Quantification brings credibility, but figures and tables can deceive, and numbers construct their own realities. What can be measured and manipulated statistically is then not only seen as real, it comes to be seen as the only or the whole reality." John Banham, of the Confederation of British Industry, said it in an equally striking way: "We are in danger of valuing most highly those things we can measure most accurately, *which means that we are often precisely wrong rather than approximately right.*"

- Pretesting, by its nature, tends to find "concerns" with creative that is out of the ordinary—thus leading to sameness and dullness.
- It defies common sense (despite the assurances of researchers) that rough storyboards, commercials and print ads can be accurately assessed. "It's like serving someone a raw leg of lamb, asking them to imagine it cooked, and then asking them how they liked it."[15]
- Research has some spectacular failures which should call in question the faith that some have in it. For example:

  ➤ The MasterCard "priceless" campaign should not have run.
  ➤ Ditto for "Heineken refreshes the parts other beers cannot reach."
  ➤ Ditto for Macintosh's 1984.
  ➤ The Seinfeld pilot got the lowest pretest score in NBC history.
  ➤ The fax machine was turned down in US group research.
  ➤ The Sony Walkman is apparently not going to succeed, but the Edsel and New Coke are.

Supporting this view, Scott Bedbury of Nike (and later Starbucks) describes the "creative client" attitude in *A New Brand World:*

> We weren't interested in trying to predict how a particular product might be received at the shopping mall, or how a new advertising campaign might be received in the living rooms of America. We didn't need, nor did we want, to pretest our creative concepts any more than we wanted to pretest Nike products. We instinctively recoiled at the notion of running a new print, radio, or TV advertisement by an ostensibly randomly selected group of consumers to find out how they might respond to it. To us, that approach lacked self-confidence and replaced gut instinct and creative intuition with conservative, risk-averse, lowest-common-denominator thinking.

Finally, and more generally, there is what we might call the "expert witness" standoff.

---

15 This is not a flip criticism. If research techniques say that "level of finish" does not make a significant difference it raises difficult questions: (a) perhaps the techniques aren't sensitive enough or (b) why is so much money subsequently spent on production values.

Those in the "no pretesting" camp don't spend their leisure time burrowing through research papers. If they did, they would be astonished at the disagreement that seethes in the academic and research communities. There are vituperative disputes about how markets and advertising work. Theories are lampooned. Study designs are crucified, or damned with faint praise. And published results are gleefully raked over the coals. This is a healthy sign of academic freedom. But it can be thought of another way.

The quantitative camp has numbers on its side. And numbers, as noted by Kestin and Vonk, beckon with the siren call of validity. In contrast, the "no research" people base their case on passion and intuition—hardly a winning strategy in a numbers-loving world.

A client may feel the magnetic pull of the numbers. But for balance, remember that the quantitative camp is not a monolith of unanimity. Behind the scenes, they look more like a loose confederation of warring tribes.

b) *The Persuasion School*[16]

Most advertising is trying to get consumers to buy or use a brand in preference to their other choices. So if someone said, "I have a technique that can predict this" they would get attention. This is what Persuasion testing (sometimes called Attitude Shift testing) claims to do.

It started with the work of Horace Schwerin in the 50s. It has since evolved into proprietary systems such as ARS and AD*Vantage. The idea is simple: find out the brand that someone prefers; show them an advertisement; find out what they now prefer. The degree of change is a measure of the advertising's persuasion. In practice (there are variations) it works like this:

An appropriate sample is invited to a theatre-type location to view a TV pilot. Before the show, they are offered a chance to win a prize in a draw. The prizes include those from the category in question. Participants indicate their favourite product, and this establishes a baseline. In the show they see the test commercial amongst others. There is another draw, and they pick their favourite product again. Any shift is presumed to trace to the ad, and can then be turned into a persuasion "score."

---

16 For this and the next section I have drawn heavily on papers by Paul Feldwick and
   Colin McDonald.

It's worth noting that the technique, in and of itself, does not have to explain why respondents have shifted from one brand to another—simply that they have. As practiced today, the suppliers do ask diagnostic questions, but the key selling feature is that the "score," pretty much as it stands, is predictive. The advocates claim a strong correlation with in-market success.

Criticism comes on many fronts, both from the "no research" school (no surprise) but also from within the academic and research community. Perhaps the most common is that it defies common sense that something as complex as advertising can be captured in such a simple—some would say simplistic—way. The whole basis of persuasion or attitude shift has also been questioned by such people as Gordon Brown and his colleagues at Millward Brown. Their thinking has its roots in ad recall and awareness, which we come to in the next section.

Brown argues that images and associations go into the memory at the time we see advertising, but that changes in attitude are likely to take place later, at the time of purchase, or after using the product. He says that a message rarely arrives at the ideal time, i.e. at purchase. From this, he concludes that attitude shift measured when we see an ad is not necessarily going to predict what will happen at the supermarket shelf etc. He also argues that the attitude shift model may not fully account for the ways that advertising works long term, to build and strengthen enduring brand perceptions.

Others have suggested that the persuasion approach works for some types of advertising/products and not others. They suggest that the technique favours brands that have new news, and that it is less hospitable to emotional appeals. It can also be seen in the data that it is harder for a big brand to get a good "score" because it starts from a higher baseline.

These are typical of the intellectual hand-grenades I referred to earlier. The advocates of persuasion testing vigorously dispute and reject these criticisms.

c) The Recall/Awareness School

The pre-post "score" in persuasion/attitude shift testing is acting as a proxy for behaviour. The recall/awareness school say that this is unrealistic. Their roots go back to Daniel Starch in the 20s, who theorized that a successful advertisement is one that is read, believed, remembered, and acted upon. Paul Feldwick notes that the techniques in this school typically measure all or most of the following:

- Impact or cut-through ability
- Recall of the brand
- Recall/comprehension of message and content
- Likes and dislikes
- Diagnostics related to believability, amusing, boring, etc.

Alex Biel describes the situation in North America as persuasion testing came on stream, and the two schools fought for supremacy:

> For over three decades, the battles between the recallers and the persuasionists were fierce and vituperative. Each side claimed that truth, beauty and sales success were theirs and theirs alone. Curiously, no other sector of the consumer research field came close to provoking the anger, zeal and "over my dead body" responses evoked by ad testing.

At one time, day-after-recall testing was the dominant pretest for TV ads in North America. But its predictive ability started to come into question, and the persuasionists came out on top, at least at this phase of the internecine war.

Meanwhile, something was happening in the UK. Millward Brown had pioneered continuous tracking, and were developing immense databases about what seemed to work and what didn't. They saw a correlation between in-market success and advertising awareness.

They developed this into the Millward Brown Advertising Awareness Index. This is not as simple as the name suggests (it is at least partly the result of statistical operations). However, it has the aura of simplicity that business hankers for. It now plays a big role in advertising evaluation in the UK, and increasingly in other markets, as Millward Brown expands.

From a predictive point of view, the Advertising Awareness Index leaves a gap, because it can only be calculated *after* a campaign has run. To fill the vacuum, Millward Brown created the LINK pretest. LINK reflects Gordon Brown's view that advertising must leave an appropriate impression in the mind, one that will resurface at the moment of purchase. The test explores various characteristics of the advertising including, as the name suggests, the linkage between the story and the brand itself. As with the persuasion tests, LINK and the Awareness Index claim a strong correlation with in-market success.

Just as the persuasion/attitude test has its detractors, so do tests such as LINK. Perhaps the sharpest criticism is that it is too "distant" from the end result of sales, relying substantially on measures of communication. This criticism is also leveled at the Awareness Index which, as noted, is based at least in part on a statistical operation—designed to "fit" the data to observed results. As with the persuasionists, Millward Brown vigorously reject the criticisms.

d) The Customizing School

It's been known for some time that strong brands combine a number of factors. I worked happily for many years with what I called the 3-D model:

© David Rutherford Strategy Consulting

Young & Rubicam have published something similar, based on the massive databases of their Brand Asset Valuator model. They found that strong brands are a combination of Relevance + Differentiation, and Knowledge + Esteem. Brands achieve this in different ways, and some researchers propose that this varies according to the role that advertising is asked to play in the marketing mix. One such proposal identifies three main paths to effectiveness:

---

17 Chapter 1 (*Positioning and All That Jazz*) explains why it says that *the brand* has to be distinctive, not necessarily the benefit.

- Persuasion
- Involvement
- Salience

A persuasion approach is probably right when you are trying to attract new users, and you have real news. An involvement approach seems more appropriate when you do not have much of a concrete nature to say, but you are appealing to people more on emotional grounds. A salience model would apply when the brand's esteem and leadership are the main drivers.

Like me in my early brand manager days, you might say "Can't I have them all" and it's true that some advertising does combine persuasion, involvement and salience. According to this line of thought, however, it is better to pick one approach, and make it the priority.

Good and Bad Research

There are many ironies in this business. One is that we are quick to say "that's a good ad" or "that's a bad ad." We far less often say the same about research, yet best practice clearly says:

> It is better to do no research than to do bad research.

But who is to know what is "good" and what is "bad"? I had an epiphany years ago when I answered a telephone survey. From the questions, it was obvious who the client was, and the answers they were looking for. At the end I said to the interviewer, "you're working for such and such, right?" She pleaded ignorance, but I persisted. Eventually, she admitted the point, signing off defiantly with, "I don't design the questions, I just ask them."

Lisa Elder touches on this in her chapter. I also suggest that next time you get that dinner-time call, tell a few fibs about what you do, and take the survey. If your experience is anything like mine, you'll be chilled by how clunky the questions are, and how your answers don't add up to how you really feel.

There are a lot of difficulties with what researchers call "hygiene." Perhaps we don't force this into the open because it would make life so very complicated. We really should.

Another Issue

Henry Ford said of the Model T, "You can have any colour you like as long as it's black." Another irony of advertising is the kaleidoscopic effort to get it right, only to have it subjected to a standard research methodology.

We know the reasons. A standardized methodology, especially in the big international advertisers, makes the whole process, well, standard. I referred earlier to the flop I caused on Campbell's. They had standardized testing. The President said to me at the time, "I know that once in a while it will misfire, but we will never learn anything if all our research is one-off."

There is an opposite view—that if you customize your research every piece of learning will be higher in quality, and over time this will accumulate to better, deeper, knowledge. I don't think these two solitudes will ever come together. I just ask clients who favour (or have to live with) standardized approaches to be empathetic to the other view—and to customize when you can.

A Final Word

As I was putting this together, I took pains to be even-handed. My test was that if the interested parties were nodding their heads and gnashing their teeth equally then I had probably achieved that objective. As to the goal of getting better decisions, I hope this chapter has done something to help.

Bibliography

It's a fascination of advertising that something so simple is so complex. Here are a dozen or so references that have caused what the diplomats call a free and frank exchange of views. If you go to these, you can start your own chain reaction by following the references that *they* give.

Baxter, M. (1999, July). "Advertising and Profitability. The Long-term Returns." *Admap*.

Buzzel, R.D., & Gale, B.T. (1987). *PIMS Principles: Linking Strategy to Performance*. New York: Free Press.

Biel, A. (1995, April). "American Developments in Advertisement Pre-testing: No Single Measure Has All the answers." *Admap*, 30(4).

Blair, M., & Rosenberg, K. (1994, May-June). "Convergent Findings Increase Our Understanding of How Ads Work." *Journal of Advertising Research*, 34(3).

Brown, G. (1991). *How Advertising Affects the Sales of Packaged Goods Brands: A Working Hypothesis for the 1990s*. Millward Brown International Plc.

Feldwick, P. (1997, June). "Agency, Client and Researcher: the Eternal Triangle." *Admap*.

Feldwick, P. (1998, January). "A Brief Guided Tour Through the Copy-Testing Jungle." *Admap*.

Haley, R., & Baldinger, A. (1991, May-June). "The ARF Copy Research Validity Project." *Journal of Advertising Research*, 31(2).

Jones, J.P. (1995). *When Ads Work: New Proof that Advertising Triggers Sales*. New York: Lexington Books.

Lodish, L., & Lubetkin, B. (1992, February). "General Truths? Nine Key Findings from the IRI Test Data." *Admap*, 27(2).

Lodish, L. (1997, September-October). "Point of View: J.P Jones and M.H Blair on Measuring Ad Effects: Another Point of View." *Journal of Advertising Research*, 37(5).

McDonald, C. (1997). "Pre-Testing Advertisements", *Admap*, Monograph # 5.

A Postscript

This chapter focused on quantitative pretesting. Lisa Elder's chapter deals with upfront qualitative, and for those interested in tracking, I recommend *Tracking Advertising and Monitoring Brands* by Colin McDonald, published by Admap.

Overview: Chapter Nine

To say that Integrated Marketing Communications is a hot topic would be an understatement. So we decided to get two views on it.

This first one is from Dr. Alan Middleton, no stranger to communication in general, and IMC in particular.

Alan worked first in marketing and advertising, closing out the practitioner part of his career as President of Enterprise Advertising (now Enterprise Creative Selling) in Toronto, and later President/CEO of JWT Japan.

Alan then transferred to academic life, and is currently Executive Director of the Division of Executive Development, and Assistant Professor of Marketing, at the Schulich School of Business, York University in Toronto.

He takes us through some of the academic underpinnings of IMC, and offers a practical approach to this challenging topic.

Chapter Nine

Integrated Marketing Communication (IMC)

DR. ALAN MIDDLETON

Introduction

The topic of Integrated Marketing Communications (IMC) causes as much discussion about what it is, as how to achieve it. Definitions are straightforward, but understanding how to apply them has turned out to be quite problematic. Wells, Burnett and Moriarty define IMC as follows:

> Integrated marketing communication (IMC) is the practice of unifying all marketing communication tools and corporate and brand messages to communicate in a consistent way to and with stakeholder audiences. IMC programs are designed to coordinate all communications messages and sources. These messages can be grouped as (a) planned (or controlled) by the company and (b) unplanned (or uncontrolled). In addition, unconsidered messages (c)—delivered by other aspects of the marketing mix (price, product and distribution) and other contact points (such as the appearance of the parking lot outside of the store)—communicate important information to stakeholders, that can negate the advertising.

> (a) advertising, sales promotion, PR, direct marketing, personal selling, point of purchase and merchandising materials, packaging, specialties, events, sponsorships, licensing, customer service, internal marketing, web site.
> (b) employee gossip and behaviour, media/government investigations, consumer group investigations, chat groups, online guerrilla sites.
> (c) facilities, service, distribution, product design and performance, price.

Based on work done on branding, including my own[1], I would suggest that alignment of the first (a) and third (c) is essential to build a strong brand. Marketing communications, however integrated, are limited in effectiveness if they suggest experiences substantially different from those delivered by the product/service, distribution and price.

The essence of IMC is that all target group touch-points deliver a coordinated and appropriate message about the brand or company. The old idea that advertising delivers one message, PR another, promotion another, direct marketing another, appropriate to the medium but without a campaign connection, is rejected by this approach. Equally, merely applying a theme line, logo or graphic to the differing vehicles is also rejected. So what is the appropriate application? This is where the controversy lies.

There seem to be three variations in the application of IMC currently.

Version I is the longer term, more data-based vision of Don Schultz, Stanley Tannenbaum and Robert Lauterman expressed in their 1994 book *Integrated Marketing Communications*. This view is that IMC should be formed around two fundamental pieces of data. The first is a full database profile of the individual customer and prospect that outlines in detail who they are demographically and psychographically, and what they think about the category and brands in the category. The second contains data on how they go about considering, choosing, buying and evaluating the brands. It thereby outlines the consumer's buying system and indicates at what points marketers might impose themselves to influence purchasing behaviour. Both of these data sets are, in their view, essential for achieving optimal IMC.

While some marketers, notably banks, telecommunications companies and some retailers, have made progress in building viable "profile" databases, they have yet to rigorously use the information to understand and take action on different individuals' buying systems. Many, if not most, marketers haven't started to build such databases. Some have found, when reviewing the lifetime customer profitability data that this detailed kind of database requires, that it was not economically viable. Does this mean that these organizations cannot engage in IMC strategy? The answer, as we shall see shortly, is no!

---

1 *Advertising Works II*—See the Bibliography.

Version II of IMC is pursued by many practitioners—representing what the brand stands for by a common "look and feel" across different communication vehicles, often by a common theme line or graphic treatment. In my view, although this is not true integrated marketing communication, it is intelligent marketing that good practitioners have been implementing for some time.[2]

There is a Version III: one that marketers and agencies can, as some already do, implement in a way that is economically viable and more effective. Version III also coordinates a range of marketing communications vehicles under a common concept or theme. However, there are two additional characteristics:

- The choice of media is based on a full understanding of the target's buying system, and not solely or primarily on the cost efficiencies of the vehicles.
- The creative material is designed not only to reflect the overall brand strategy, but also the specific role the media vehicle has in the target's buying system.

This is a good, and I believe, realistic, approach. It is also in line with the approach taken by the American Marketing Association in Larry Percy's book *Strategies for Implementing Marketing Communications*, which provides some pragmatic and actionable models to help the reader implement IMC planning.

---

2 In my practitioner life I was involved in several examples. UK 1968, The House of Elida: a range of women's hair products (shampoos, hairsprays, colorants, styling aids) where not only advertising, packaging, and promotion materials were coordinated, but there was a full PR program to train and motivate store assistants. UK 1970, the launch of the Access credit card: the advertising agency was responsible for naming and designing the card, employing resources to train the merchant force, identifying and signing up stores, advertising, all collateral material, direct mail, PR, consumer and retailer promotion—all under a consistent theme. Canada 1977–1981, The Pepsi Challenge: this was not just advertising, but direct mail, in-mall and event sampling, sponsorship, and PR, with all material developed and themed on a phase-by-phase basis. Japan 1989–1991, De Beers diamonds: the advertising agency was in charge of retailer training and promotion, general event PR, advertising, promotional events, and direct mail.

The Importance of IMC

Why should anyone pay attention to IMC? What is wrong with continuing to have the agency do the advertising, the promotion house do the promotion, and the DM house do the internet or other direct marketing—without more than a cursory reference to each other's work or the overall strategy or target group buying system? Let's remind ourselves of some marketing communication principles to establish why IMC is important and how it can be approached.

1. We know that people buy goods and services by combining information from memory with impressions formed at the moment of consideration and/or purchase (the situational influences).
2. While getting people to buy solely from situational influences is achievable, persuading people to form brand preferences, and an attitudinal as well as behavioural loyalty, requires a memory response as well.
3. The long-term memory stores impressions of a brand and its associations together with an evaluative component. Strong brands come easily to mind. These brand impressions often create a predisposition to buy that is so strong that it will overcome any situational influences. With well-managed brands, the situational influences are reviewed in the most favourable light. With less well-managed brands these impressions and associations will be weaker.
4. To get things stored in long-term memory needs a certain consistency of message—not sameness, but consistency.
5. In getting communication stored in long-term memory, mere repetition is overrated. It is clear in research that repetition of the same message in the same medium is not the most effective way to build long-term memory. This does not mean that messages should be unrelated. In fact they *must* be.
6. Communication around the same concept or theme, done in different ways via differing vehicles, is very much more powerful than repetition of exactly the same message in one medium, and the likelihood is higher that the brand and its associations will move into long term memory.

7. Getting brand communications into long-term memory also requires a strong emotional response,[3] what one scholar has called "having (such) significant and emotional impact to leave a synaptic trace in the memory."

8. Great brands, those that achieve lower price elasticity and higher levels of attitudinal and behavioural loyalty and therefore higher brand equity, have achieved strong brand awareness and associations in long-term memory.

IMC and Target Group Differences

So far we have talked about memory and response to situational influences as if these are universal responses. In one way they are. In a very important way, they are not.

When we discuss what we know about the physiological processes of the brain, we are discussing universal responses. However, when we examine how these universal responses result in market behaviour, we are struck by the importance of individual and segment differences.

Buying behaviour is complex because of the sheer number of influences that impact how we store things in memory, and how we balance memory versus situational influences in our decision-making.

First there are Environmental Influences. These include cultural background, ethnic background, social class, family, household, and peer group influences.

Then there are Individual Differences. These include the mental resources to comprehend communication, and the physical and financial resources to respond to it. They include previous knowledge the individual has about the category, brand and competitors. They include previous and current attitudes. They include what type of personality, values and lifestyle the individual has or relates to. And they include how the individuals see themselves and how motivated they are by the category and the brands in it.

---

3 Batra and Ray in 1986 listed 15 types of affect (emotion): interest/expectancy, surprise, disgust/scorn, skepticism, anger, fear/anxiety, shame, guilt, pity, pride, sadness, social affection, drives (e.g. pain, fatigue), deactivation (or quiet pleasure), and what they call SEVA—surgency, elation, vigour, and activation (active joy).

This aspect of motivation is the Involvement Level, and it's critical to the buying system, which has classically been conceptualized as: need recognition – search – prepurchase evaluation – purchase – consumption – satisfaction – postpurchase evaluation – repeat or new purchase.

While for years economists assumed this was the way all people purchased all goods and services, consumer and business research shows otherwise. Often, buyers skip stages and go straight from need recognition to purchase. Or purchase out of impulse. Or do with only a very restricted search and evaluation.

The involvement concept is often misunderstood. It does not apply to goods or services, but to *the individual buyer.* Buying a car may be very involving for one individual: who gets data from the internet and brochures from the dealer, watches car ads, and talks to friends and salespeople before making a decision. To another, it may be very uninvolving. He or she just buys the same as before, or does what feels good. The same person, though, may be deeply involved in choosing a toothpaste—considering fluoride, taste, packaging, availability and price, because it is a key part of the overall health and hygiene of the family.

All of these differences and influences cause the role of memory and situational influence to vary. As such, they need to be understood segment by segment, or even individual by individual if possible. Then, communication needs to be consistency segment by segment. The marketer also needs to ensure that communication for one segment does not contradict what is aimed at another, if it will be seen by more than one segment.

In short, in order to register impressions in long-term memory we need to understand how different target groups respond to different stimuli. Additionally, we need to achieve appropriate and coordinated impressions across the broad range of planned *and* unconsidered sources that impact these different target groups—those diverse sources in the definitions at the beginning of this chapter.

IMC and Marketplace Reality

The difficulty of achieving coordination and consistency across a broad range of communications is compounded by two realities of the marketplace.

First, there is the tendency of marketers to send out differing messages in differing media because marketing communications are handled by different people, who in turn deal with different suppliers. In very few organizations is the responsibility for coordinating what Wells, Burnett and Moriarty called "planned messages" in one place. In virtually none is coordination with the rest of the marketing mix (the "unconsidered messages") in one place. This lack of coordination—built into the structure of organizations—influences how any communications strategy is executed. It makes coordination very difficult.

This lack of coordination is not only latitudinal, not only a problem with the communication mix at any one point in time. What may be worse is that the problem is longitudinal, in how the mix is planned and evolved over time. In current planning and thinking, I observe very little of the consistent longitudinal brand-meaning management that is so essential for building positive impressions in long-term memory, and therefore strong brands.

The second reality is what I call the "three fragmentations in marketing." In the last twenty to thirty years we have seen three huge shifts:

- *Target group fragmentation.* As basic needs and wants are met, marketers shift to those that are more specific to certain segments, and then to those even more niche. Marketers know that the more tightly defined a target group, the more satisfactorily they can meet their needs and wants, the lower the price sensitivity, and the greater the profitability. Many marketers have seized this opportunity to target more specific and narrower segments. In this way the target groups have fragmented.
- *Distribution systems fragmentation.* As our fragmented target groups seek to source their goods and services from locations convenient to them, and not just the manufacturer or retailer, so distribution fragments. Grocery stores no longer just sell groceries, but financial services. Drug stores sell electronics. The specialist stores get bigger. Buyers can buy online or offline through the "bricks and clicks." Buyers can buy through paper or electronic catalogues. And goods and services can be delivered directly to the desired location.

- *Communications fragmentation.* Communication with these fragmenting groups is itself fragmenting. Fifty years ago, the major programs in broadcast (TV or radio) and the major titles in print
  (magazines and newspapers) would reach a majority of any target
  group with enough frequency to convey a powerful branding message. As broadcast moved to narrowcast, as mass magazines and
  newspapers moved to special interest, as entertainment choices
  broadened to include videotape, then video disk, then download-
  able music, programs and information, and as street-based media
  took hold, the media world fragmented—and it continues to do so.

These three fragmentations mean that marketers increasingly have different messages in different places encouraging people to buy from
different types of distribution outlet. The problem is how to integrate
communications across this ever-increasing range of target groups, distribution outlets and media.

The market is pushing for more precise targeting and therefore more
knowledge of how to use different communications vehicles, *and* how
to integrate.

Organizations have tended to respond by developing expertise and
structures specific to the communication product—advertising, database marketing, PR, sponsorship promotion and so on. Mostly, they
have not developed the expertise for managing brand meaning and
target group relationships over media and over time—in other words,
expertise in integrated marketing communications.

Implementation: Media and Creative Implications
for the User/Buyer Target Groups

We have seen what integrated marketing communications is, how it is
wrongly and rightly applied, and why it is important. We have also
seen why it might be difficult to implement. We now need to spend a
little time indicating how a marketer goes about achieving a better
integration of marketing and marketing communication effort.

First, we will consider the user or buyer of goods and services and
how we achieve better integration of our communication to them.

Underlying the planning of IMC is the target group buying system.
Simply stated, IMC works best by understanding the target group's
attitudes and behaviours regarding the category and brand, understanding their involvement, identifying the changes in the buying

system that will have the highest leverage against the brand objective, then determining what messages—delivered how, when, and where— can achieve the desired objective.

Good marketers already do much of this. The difference of IMC, versus merely taking a campaign theme to differing media based on media reach, frequency and cost efficiency, lies in the two things mentioned briefly a little earlier:

- the choice of media is based on analysis of the buying system, to deliver the greatest influence at the points of highest leverage
- the creative message will be strategically and conceptually similar, but each medium will have creative developed to optimize the message, *and* the role of the medium, *and* its contribution to the target's buying system.

Media Choice

Currently, the tendency is to choose media based on cost efficiency, target group reach and frequency, and the often persuasive viewpoints of vendors, whether it be online advertising, event sponsorship, trade show and so on. In IMC, the media considered are those that impact the points of most leverage in the target's buying system, changing attitude or behaviour in favour of the brand.

For example, in a launch, before spending large sums on advertising, it may be necessary to spend against sampling and trial-inducing activities in promotion and PR. (We know that advertising works best when it reinforces impressions from direct experience with a product or service.) With a service provider like a bank or a retailer, before spending money on target group communications, it may be necessary to spend money training and communicating product knowledge to employees. (We know that the service customers receive is far more powerful in forming impressions of the brand than advertising alone.) In relaunching an existing brand, investment in the brands product and image through R&D and advertising may be far more important than co-op retailer funds.

There are, of course, some major problems in making these determinations with appropriate accountability and measurement.

Decisions are hampered by two things. First, there is no common measurement system to weigh the relative contributions of a TV campaign versus a street-based sampling versus an opinion leader adoption campaign versus a trade show versus investment in an upgraded web site versus a point-of-purchase campaign with a direct mail drop. In this situation:

- be clear about the role in the buying system the media is to fulfill, and measure its contribution against those objectives.
- test the chosen media against a mix elsewhere that does not include it. While test marketing may have gone out of favour due to slow results and competitive intelligence, there is no reason to avoid constant testing and modeling of differing media mixes. It is unlikely that a competitor's intelligence system is so finely tuned as to detect media mix tests.

The second problem is who will evaluate the media. The way the industry is structured now, there is no group that routinely evaluates media in its broadest sense. Media buying groups have difficulties dealing with comparisons between the five traditional media of TV, radio, magazine, newspaper and outdoor, let alone the myriad of other communications that touch a target group.

The solution is for marketers to work with their suppliers to develop measurement and evaluation systems that can be refined based on the input of research over time. Only by measuring will we learn, and only by learning will we improve.

These are not perfect solutions to the problems, but they are achievable. In times of great changes when old rules no longer apply, guidelines that are tested through experience are the best we can hope for. So:

- Map out your target group's buying system.
- Determine where the brand stands in the system (including involvement level).
- Determine your realistic objectives.
- Decide at what points in the buying system you should concentrate activity.
- Review the available media at those points and choose the vehicles to use, based on effectiveness and efficiency measures.
- Develop appropriate creative (see next section).
- Execute.

- Research.
- Review.
- Refine.

Those who would like a useful format for this process should refer to the Budget Allocation Grid suggested in Chapter 7 of the Larry Percy book referred to earlier.

Creative Approaches

Currently, two approaches tend to occur. In one there is a lead supplier, often the advertising agency, who develops the creative for the advertising campaign in traditional media. Once this is close to completion, the work is given to other specialist suppliers who try to adapt it to their medium. I call this the "advertising-dominant approach."

There are two problems with this. Not only does it assume that advertising is the dominant approach in the target group's buying system (which is not always valid), it also assumes that creative executed in broadcast and print are automatically appropriate for other media. Sadly this is not always the case, which is why one sees so much communication with a theme line and logo sitting awkwardly on materials clearly not designed to be used in this way.

The second approach is where the supplier, again often the advertising agency, recognizes that other media need to be used, e.g. direct mail, and applies the advertising execution to that other medium. The problem here is that the supplier is often making the unconsidered assumption that the other media have the same role in the customer's buying and consideration system as the advertising. Also, they may not have sufficient skills in the other media.

While thinking about the application of creative work in all relevant media should be encouraged, it is often not IMC, but stretching an execution designed for one medium to fit others. It results in the problems outlined above, and I call this the "pseudo-IMC approach." (In case there are those who think I am unfairly criticizing agencies, let me say that the sin is equal when a PR, Internet or DM supplier produces ideas that are just dropped into advertising or point-of-sale materials, or when an advertiser orders this to happen without thinking through the consequences.)

There is a third way that some are pursuing. It is the "real-IMC" way, and it has two forms.

- In one, a lead marketing communications agency develops a media-neutral *concept* for test, then the concept is taken by the differing specialists for development into their particular medium—based on clear buying system roles and objectives. Media neutral formats for testing include concept boards, postcards or billboards, with the concept communicated by a key visual and a copy line.
- In the other, all communications suppliers are briefed simultaneously. Then each comes up with campaign concept and, working with the best (chosen by research and judgment), all translate the central concept to their medium by working in partnership with the other suppliers.

This third way forces the various practitioners to develop and understand the difference between a marketing communications campaign concept and a media-specific execution.

Great communication concepts are just that. They are ideas based on insights into the brand-consumer relationship. These have the power and flexibility to be adapted to many differing types of marketing communications media. Media- specific executions—a TV approach, a DM approach, and so on—have their role, but often lack the power to build strong brands.

With this IMC discipline, therefore, an added advantage will be felt—a more focused effort to express the brand positioning and benefits in different media, rather than making do with less powerful executions specific to certain media.

Either of the "real-IMC" approaches are more difficult to manage than the "advertising-dominant" or "pseudo-IMC" approaches, but are likely to be more effective in creating relevant consumer touchpoints, and therefore in building attitudinal and behavioural brand loyalty. Creative done in this form, therefore, has three components:

- Across all media there must be a powerful and shared underlying strategy and concept that positions the brand and its benefits against competitors.

- The concept or idea must be adapted to each medium, to address the role it plays in the target group's buying system. If the role is to stimulate immediate purchase then the creative execution had better convey a sense of urgency. If it is a brochure in a dealership, then it should not only convey information in a persuasive manner, but invite interaction with available staff. And so on.
- The adapted creative must suit the specific media. It must be designed to use the strengths of the medium and its interrelationship with the target consumer.

Some media can be used in different ways by consumers. A web site can, for instance, be both a quick simple communicator, and an involving, informing one. The design chosen must be based on an understanding of the target group's involvement level. Whatever decision is made, however, the creative must work optimally in the context of the medium chosen. This may all sound obvious, but sadly the test of observation of our marketplaces suggests a poor ability to execute it. We see all too often:

- Creative designed for impact in media used for understanding.
- Creative that uses :30 TV wonderfully, but gives no additional understanding of the brand in 60 seconds of radio.
- Creative designed for image media used for direct response (and vice versa).
- Creative designed for attitude change in sponsorship vehicles best suited to user reinforcement.

To avoid the harm done by this kind of undisciplined approach, a real-IMC approach based on the target group's buying system needs to be adopted.

Implementation: Understanding the Buying Group

So far we have discussed the impact of IMC against a traditional target group. Contemporary practitioner and academic research points up the narrowness of this idea. In the following sections we will discuss target group influencers and company employees, but first we need to examine who does the buying in B2C and B2B groups.

The sometimes overt but always tacit model in the West has been that individuals are the unit for focus as user or buyer. The model has recognized the importance of influencers, but has explicitly or implicitly relegated them to secondary status. Recent research, in the B2C world, points up how much of the interaction between influencer and buyer in the family, peer group, or other buying group, is in essence shared decision making and must be examined as such.

For example, there has been a great deal of study of the "kidfluence" on family purchase. So much so that the question is whether this is influence or actually shared decision-making. Whatever it is, it is hugely influential. Similar questions can be raised around large family purchases like cars, vacations, houses and the like. When people go through life-stage changes—such as living together, the arrival of children and so on—the same questions arise, as they do with peer group influenced purchases like beer, soft drinks, and fashion. Also, in many ethnic groups in our society, the group decision model applies to a whole range of goods and services.

B2B transactions are already recognized by most marketers as buying-group driven, and mostly managed as such. The point is that in many B2C and B2B cases decision-making may be shared, and should be managed as such, researched as such, understood as such, and communicated as such. In these cases, IMC takes on the additional meaning of integration across all people in the decision group.

Implementation: "Network Hub" Target Groups

The term "network hubs" may not be familiar, but the idea behind it will be. To quote Kotler, Jain, and Maesincee in *Marketing Moves:*

> Network hubs are individuals who communicate with more people about a certain market offering than the average person does. Other terms for network hubs are opinion leaders, influencers, lead users and power users. Network hubs may not be the first to adopt new products, but they have a great influence on future purchases.

These are the Influentials whose word-of-mouth, buzz, purchases and/or opinions are sought in this increasingly networked age.

The interest in this aspect of communication comes from a rediscovery of adoption and diffusion theory first developed by University of Chicago sociologists in the 30s. It was revived in the 60s by Everett Rogers in his *Diffusion of Innovations* work that you know as the adoption curve: innovators, early adopters, early majority, late majority and laggards, and in the late 90s as buzz marketing, viral marketing and the like.

Network hub target groups are crucially important as many consumers are increasingly shutting out traditional forms of marketing communication in favour of trusting their own networks.

Every consumer or business buyer has networks of contacts. Some of these are highly influential, especially in some markets. Kotler, Jain, and Maesincee point out that with some products that lend themselves to high consumer involvement, this is a particularly important communications channel. Also, with certain target groups, most evidently with relatively homogeneous, high-contact groups like preteens, teenagers, doctors, lawyers, and farmers, this is a particularly powerful channel. The challenge with these groups is not only to identify the networks, and the Influentials in the networks, but how to communicate with them. So many marketers are clumsily trying to influence these people directly. The response is increasing rejection and hostility.

Subtlety and patience is more promising—allowing the influencer to experience the product/service without overt pressure. The point is that the style of this channel of communication needs to be integrated into the other activities. This network hub communication may become the primary marketing communications channel of the next decades. At minimum, unless actively considered, it will become a key weakness in any integrated marketing communications strategy.

Implementation: Internal Marketing—Employees

With over 70% of our economy in service industries it is not surprising that many, if not most, customer-brand relationships are primarily formed around service—interaction with an organization through contact with its employees.

True IMC means that employees are not only a target group in and of themselves, they are a critical element in the customer's experience, just as Wells, Burnett and Moriarty suggested in their definition at the beginning of this chapter.

In many organizations, employee communications are thought of as separate from marketing communications activity, and are the job of the HR Department or the Corporate Communications group. An internal newsletter is produced, internal memos are sent, and picnics and staff sports events facilitated. The strategy for employees is driven by other than customer considerations.

In successful organizations, employee communication is the first stop on the path to IMC. There is a crossover between training and communication. Employees need to understand a company's policies, products and processes. They also need training in how to apply this information, and how to serve customers. This combination of communications and training must accomplish three things:

- Well ahead of publicly announcing a new campaign, product, initiative or brand promise, a full program of briefings, training and communication is needed. This includes a full background behind the development, and most importantly, the part the employee has to play. In exactly the same way as IMC media are chosen to impact on the appropriate points in the consumer buying system, so the employee activity should be chosen.
- There should be ongoing training and communication to show employees how they must contribute to the brand promise. This is not just informing employees once a year of the company objectives, financial targets and behavioural targets, but fully briefing them on the brand's promise and their role in fulfilling it. This requires training and communication in three areas:

  1. The brand-promise, and why it creates a compelling distinctive position in the marketplace
  2. Product knowledge, knowledge of processes and systems for when they or the customer need it, and customer contact training
  3. Measurement and feedback so that improvement is constantly encouraged

- The program must include all customer contact personnel and *their* support systems and people. Too often, even the limited training and communication that takes place is aimed only at direct customer contact personnel. This is not adequate. Finance and IT departments not only enable improved customer service, they often have direct contact with the customer. The same is true of many internal departments. In the 80s Northwestern Airlines in the US improved their customer relations not by only training the ground and air host personnel, but by improving their on-time record through an aggressive program of training and communication to their maintenance staff. Marriott Hotels train their employees, whatever their job, to assist guests when asked, and not pass it off to someone else. The goal is to align all employee effort around the brand promise.

In a networked, service economy, employees must be seen as important customers, opinion leaders and customer-loyalty facilitators. As such they merit the same rigor and planning of communications as the customer. The senior manager of a large Japanese automotive company said it well, "Employee care and customer care are two sides of the same coin." (Toyama-san of Nissan). They must know and understand what the organization is intending for the brand, first. They must be listened to and allowed to input to plans and strategies. They are, after all, the front-line carrier of the brand promise in many if not most contemporary industries.

Implementation: Some Useful Formats for Planning

In *Strategies for Implementing Integrated Marketing Communications* Larry Percy provides useful formats to help implement and discipline the IMC process. The first, the "Behavioural Sequence Model" (BSM) outlines the major decision stages the target group might use, then examines the details of these decisions, the location where they are made, the timing and how they will occur. The second, the "IMC Task Grid", links this BSM to possible IMC actions. In addition to these formats, Percy gives cases of application that can help the reader develop their own approaches. For those serious about IMC application, this book is well worth sourcing.

A Final Brief Note on Other Target Groups

This chapter has focused on IMC around the customer. However, there are other target groups, and while the core of the brand promise should be the same or very similar, its adaptation will vary depending on the nature of the target group and the benefits the organization wants to offer them.

These stakeholders include shareholders, and particularly the pension funds and investment community. They include bureaucrats and politicians. They include advocacy groups engaged in another aspect of the political process. The media will be targets, as will local, national or international community groups.

Against all of these groups, the basic brand promise needs to be similar, but focused in a way appropriate for the target group. But it must be integrated so that whoever the target group, the same fundamental identity emerges.

IMC: Summary of Key Issues

In this chapter only the bare bones of IMC have been discussed. The intent is to give some principles and guidelines. These can be summarized as:

- A real IMC approach requires detailed knowledge of the target group. Not only who they are—how they relate to the brand, where the strengths and weaknesses are versus competition and the ideal— but also their involvement level and buying system, and the points to focus on.
- The marketer uses this knowledge to develop a brand communications strategy.
- This strategy has two components—latitudinal and a longitudinal. The latitudinal component uses the target's buying system to determine media choice in the short term (roughly one year). The longitudinal component determines what aspects of the brand's reputation to focus on in the short, medium and long term—in other words, how brand meaning is managed.
- In the short term, the latitudinal component, media and creative are selected to (1) carry the central concept across all media, (2) be adapted to the specific task in the buying system, (3) provide a seamless connection across media.
- In an increasingly networked consumer world, IMC must focus on two important additional groups—Network Hubs, and Employees. These must be included in any IMC plan for it to be truly effective.

The benefit is a more systematic development of the brand's value to its target group, and therefore to its owner. It may be difficult to implement and manage. It may take rethinking and reorganization. But, in a highly competitive world, IMC is increasingly an essential approach to achieving that greatest of corporate assets, a strong brand.

Selected Bibliography

Aaker, D., & Biel A. (1993). *Brand Equity and Advertising*. Hillsdale, N.J: Lawrence Erlbaum Associates.

Belch, G., Belch, M., & Guolla, M. (2003). *Advertising and Promotion: An Integrated Marketing Communications Perspective*. Whitby, ON: McGraw Hill Ryerson.

Burnett, J., Moriarty, S., & Grant S. E. (2001). *Introduction to Integrated Marketing Communications*. Toronto: Prentice Hall.

Broadbent, S. (1989). *The Advertising Budget : the Advertiser's Guide to Budget Determination*. Oxon: NTC Publications.

Clow, K.E., & Baack, D. (2002). *Integrated Advertising, Promotion and Marketing Communications*. Upper Saddle River, N.J. : Prentice Hall.

Duncan, T. (2002). *IMC – Using Advertising and Promotion to Build Brands*. Boston: McGraw Hill.

Franzen, G. (1994). *Advertising Effectiveness: Findings from Empirical Research*. Oxfordshire U.K. : NTC Publications.

Gad, T. (2001). *4-D Branding: Cracking the Corporate Code of the Network Economy*. London: Financial Times/Prentice Hall.

Hill, S., & Lederer, C. (2001). *The Infinite Asset: Managing Brands to Build New Value*. Boston, Mass.: Harvard Business School.

Jones, J.P. ed. (1999). *How to Use Advertising to Build Strong Brands*. Thousand Oaks, Calif.: Sage.

Jones, J.P. ed. (1998). *How Advertising Works: The Role of Research*. Thousand Oaks, Calif.: Sage.

Jones, J.P. (1995). *When Ads Work: New Proof that Advertising Triggers Sales*. New York: Lexington Books.

Jones, J.P. (1992). *How Much is Enough?: Getting the Most from your Advertising Dollar*. New York: Lexington Books.

Jones, J.P. (1986). *What's in a Name: Advertising and the Concept of Brands*. Lexington Mass.: Lexington Books.

Kitchen, P.J. (1999). *Marketing Communications: Principles and Practice*. London: International Thomson Business Press.

Kotler, P., Jain, D., & Suvit, M. (2002). *Marketing Moves: A New Approach to Profits, Growth, and Renewal*. Boston: Harvard Business School Press.

McDonald, C. (1992). *How Advertising Works: A Review of Current Thinking.* Oxfordshire, U.K.: NTC Publications.

Middleton A. C., & Dalla Costa J. (1997). *Advertising Works II.* Toronto: Institute of Canadian Advertising.

Percy L. (1997). *Strategies for Implementing Integrated Marketing Communications.* Lincolnwood, Ill: NTC Business Books.

Schultz, D.E, Tannenbaum, S.I., & Lauterborn, R.F. (1994). *Integrated Marketing Communications.* Lincolnwood, Ill.: NTC Books.

Semenik, R.J. (2002). *Promotion and Integrated Marketing Communications.* Cincinnati, OH: Southwestern/Thomson Learning.

Sirgy, M.J. (1998). *Integrated Marketing Communications: A Systems Approach.* Upper Saddle River, N.J: Prentice Hall.

Smith, P.R. (2000). *Marketing Communications: An Integrated Approach.* London: Kogan Page.

Smith, P.R., Berry, C., & Pulford, A. (2000). *Strategic Marketing Communications: New Ways to Build and Integrate Communication.* London: Kogan Page.

Solomon, M.R, Zaichkowsky, J.L, & Polegato, R. (1999). *Consumer Behavior: Buying Having and Being.* Scarborough, ON: Prentice Hall Canada.

Wells, W., Burnett, J., & Moriarty, S.E. (2000). *Advertising Principles and Practice.* Englewood Cliffs, N.J.: Prentice Hall.

Wind, Y., Mahajan, V., & Gunther, R.E. (2002). *Convergence Marketing: Running with the Centaurs.* Upper Saddle River, N.J: Financial Times Prentice Hall.

Overview: Chapter Ten

This chapter, like Chapter 9, is also about Integrated Marketing Communication, but this time from the practical point of view. Laurie Young and Guy Stevenson describe how IMC is handled at Ogilvy.

They discuss the minefields that make this seemingly simple idea difficult to put into practice, and give several suggestions for success.

I can remember a time when one of the main beliefs of IMC was that there had to be a consistent "look and feel" across all effort. This was often taken to mean that the visuals and slogans of one medium had to appear in all of them. This explains why some IMC effort clumsily misfires.

This chapter says that force-feeding an idea from one medium into another is not the right way to go. Each medium should be used in the way it works best. How, then, do you keep the total effort connected and consistent? By having it adhere to a more embracing concept than look and feel. At Ogilvy, they call it The Organizing Idea.

There is also a caveat. IMC will not work if the agency and client continue to work in the old silo set-up. It needs structural and attitudinal change to break down those walls. This is something to bear in mind as you read on.

Chapter Ten

IMC—A View from the Front Lines

LAURIE YOUNG AND GUY STEVENSON

Introduction

Not that long ago, Integrated Marketing Communication was in its infancy. It sounded like the right thing to do—in the sense that having effort aligned is surely better than having it march to different drummers—but for various reasons it was hard to put it into practice.

Today, although there are still challenges, it is becoming the price of entry.

Like so much in our business, there's confusion over definitions. Some come at IMC with attitudes they have inherited from their particular discipline, simply overlaid with the need to "get the same look and feel into everything we do." Others (e.g. Don Shultz, a leading academic and consultant, and one of the pioneers of IMC) envisage a marketplace driven by immense databanks of consumer information. Still others (and that includes Ogilvy) have an approach that is neither of these, though it has aspects of both.

In this approach, the central idea is to think about every point of contact with the consumer. Equally key is *not* to see communication in the narrow media sense. Contact could just as likely be word of mouth from a friend, the impression created by a billing statement, how you are treated on the phone or in a showroom, the feel of the pack when you pick it up, and so on. In other words, a brand isn't what we *communicate*—it's what the consumer *experiences*. Consumers don't differentiate by channel of communication; it's all one brand regardless how they experience it.

In this sense, the "C" of IMC is a misnomer. Consumers build relationships with brands, and this manifests itself beyond any narrow definition of communication. Of course, not all touch-points have the same weight. Some will be nice to have. Some are so powerful they help a consumer decide to stay or leave a franchise. These are Moments of Truth.

Consistency of brand idea and behaviour is critical at Moments of Truth. If the brand is about service, the frontline staff need to embrace it, and deliver it.[1] If you invest huge amounts building an image for your brand, you don't want a badly handled customer service call to lead to a 67% defection rate.[2] Corporate actions, big and small, must reflect the brand promise. At every point of contact. At all times. To every audience.

At Ogilvy we call this 360 Degree Brand Stewardship.

The Importance of IMC in a Complex Marketplace

Integrated messaging helps make sense of a fragmented marketplace.

It offers familiarity and no surprises. ("I know what to expect.") It offers ease. ("It's shorthand, so I make choices faster.") This routine or ritual almost always favours the known over the unknown. This doesn't mean being boring or too comfortable. Think of Virgin: hip, innovative, adventurous, fresh, moving into categories where these values thrive, and offer competitive advantage. Different agencies produce the advertising for their airline, mobile phone, and credit card, but it is all very Virgin in values and character. So is everything else that they do. It's a compelling brand vision perpetrated through integrated marketing.

IMC goes further than simply making it easier for consumers. It is a powerful tool that makes the whole greater than the sum of the parts, through impact and efficiency. There's an adage "friends don't shout loud to be heard." Through consistency the brand's message becomes more motivating and memorable, if we've done our job right and made the promise clear and relevant.

---

1 An example from the Hall of Infamy is "We Hurry" for Gulf gas stations. The decidedly unhurried pump jockeys didn't realize that the words referred to them.

2 From the work of The Henley Centre, Blackfriars, London—a leading European Strategic Consultancy.

What's the Catch?

In a few words, IMC is *really tough to do*. Here are the four big land-mines, followed by some thoughts on how to avoid them.

a) Landmine One—What Exactly is The Brand?

No point is more hotly debated. We found an article claiming that Plato was the first to articulate the importance of a brand's essence, because he believed that deep within everything concrete is the idea of that thing.[3]

It's ironic that what should be an enabler often proves to be a trap. After all, the Brand is a higher entity than any of the activities that help create it. Higher than a brilliant strategic insight. Higher than an advertising campaign (however effective). Higher than a Direct Marketing campaign with an ROI off the charts. Higher than an interactive campaign that attracts consumers like bees to the honeypot. This should surely help integration. But because the Brand is a collection of experiences, expectations, feelings and values, it's hard to wrestle it into an expression that works across disciplines. And there's no consistency in that expression anyway.[4]

The many "brand" ideas exist because a brand is a collection of some pretty intangible concepts. Even among people from the same discipline this is a recipe for extensive debate. With several disciplines involved, interpretations increase exponentially. People in general advertising[5] tend to think in terms of the brand's relationship with the consumer, and look for the single-most important key to that relationship. People from Direct have a more transactional model. People from Interactive or Promotion or PR have a different view again. Sometimes the sticking point is the role of Emotional versus Rational. Sometimes it will turn on whether you have found the "truth" of the Brand. Whatever the issue, the debate can eat up days of development time.

---

3   See Chapter One, where it appears that GOD was the first Brand Manager. It seems that Plato was the first Planner.

4   We're talking about Brand Essence, Brand Equity, Brand Truth etc. but also approaches like brand manifestos, brand films, brand stories.

5   There is no single word for what used to be called advertising. We are using "general" to distinguish from Direct Marketing, Interactive, PR etc.

Let's say you reach (apparent) consensus. The general advertising people have their notion as to what it implies. The DR, Interactive, Promotion and PR guys have theirs. They agree with the planner on how it can fit together. Work begins.

Then you find that the work, in the hands of the writers and art directors in the various disciplines, can vary wildly. How *do* you best imbue notions like femininity, prestige and sociability? And when it comes to values—for example integrity or non-conformity—the job becomes even more difficult. We've all been there. Stay tuned.

b) Landmine Two—The Channels

What channel is best for getting the message to the various targets?

Different channels have different strengths and weaknesses. General advertising (even long-copy print) usually works best when a single-minded idea drives the brand story. It influences our attitude towards the brand down the road, at the point of purchase—at the grocery store, when we need car repairs, when seeking a mortgage, and so on. Direct Response advertising is designed to elicit a response right away. Now, not later, it wants you to pick up the phone, fill out the application, sign up on the net. In contrast to the "single idea" at the heart of general advertising, response levels are driven by information. Lots of it.

There is no easy way to meld these realities. Shoehorning DR techniques into general advertising will reduce its effectiveness, and uncritically importing "the idea" from general advertising to DR will damage response rates.

The internet adds another layer of complexity. It's idea driven like general advertising, but also content driven like direct marketing. It had immediate interactivity like the phone, and the unique ability to measure real-time response. This is very different from other channels. Plus, there is the touchy issue that the "toys" web designers love to use may not fit the essence of the brand.

Promotion has its own complexities. How do you deal with the fact that the best pull for a Sweepstakes may come from offering Money, Houses, and Cars—but the Brand Character calls for a visit to a knitting factory?

None of this is new news, but you have to reconcile these different points of view. You have to achieve consistency (across every point of contact and over time) in what the brand stands for, what it promises, and how it delivers that promise.

c) Landmine Three—The Targets

Many brands have multiple targets.

A packaged goods brand may be targeted at some combination of Moms, Dads, Kids, Teens, Tweens. It could also target health professionals, or food service operators, or some other atypical group. High-ticket items will aim at consumers, but often have to appeal to store personnel as well. In fast food and similar markets, the franchisees are a crucial audience.

Creating the right kind of consistency across all these groups is a lot more than cutting and pasting imagery from one discipline to the others. Often, the problem isn't with the end audiences at all. The true challenge is to manage the silos at the client, and on the agency side.

d) Landmine Four—Getting the Brand Touch-points to Ring True

Dodging Landmines One to Three still leaves what we believe is fundamental to successful IMC—that "communication" shouldn't just be about the ads we create, the mail we send, the splash page we mount, or the promotion we run:

> Every Brand Touch-point[6] needs to reflect the brand in
> a way that rings completely true.

Finding A Smoother Path

We can't claim to have discovered how to manoeuvre around all the obstacles to delivering IMC. But there are some pretty challenging cases in the Ogilvy scrapbook, and the experience has helped us codify some principles.

---

6   This is the Ogilvy term for every point of contact.

The most fundamental steps are not about the consumer—they are organizational. With these in place, IMC is easier to think through, and far less time is wasted on territorial issues. Better effort gets to the marketplace, and this effort can be continuously improved.

a) Leadership

In the agency, it starts at the top, with senior management endorsement. It takes a heartfelt respect for the brand, and all the disciplines that help build it—not the attitude that IMC is a necessary evil, or a way to generate more profit. It's critical to have one Brand Director. He or she will have roots in one discipline, but needs to be fluent enough in the others to recognize opportunities and issues. This leader must be media neutral, with nothing but the best possible business result at heart. Too many chiefs will guarantee failure. It's ideal if the client also has one chief.[7]

b) One Common P&L

Infighting will kill any hope of successful IMC. From our experience, a common P&L for the brand (not each discipline) is non-negotiable. The brand's interests come first. Full stop. If the current structure doesn't allow this, change it. Or risk a stream of half successes and outright failures. In a structural sense, this also applies to clients. Silos are destructive. The need to break them down was by far the most frequently mentioned challenge in a recent survey on integrated marketing[8] by www.reveries.com.

c) Planning

This isn't wicked strategies or creative briefs, but getting all disciplines to the table up front, and being media neutral in answering how we want our target (s) to respond to our message.

---

7   Ogilvy, like many agencies, has all or most disciplines under one roof. But as Alan Middleton points out, services can also come from different companies. Either way, it is *essential* to have an experienced, brand-driven, media-neutral leader.

8   Entitled "How's It Integrating?"

It will start with input from all disciplines, but the final allocation of funds must be based on a combination of bottom-up planning, historical in-market experience, and the marketing goal.

The team works with the understanding that each channel is better at certain jobs than others. Basically, what are the jobs to be done, and what combinations of channels will most successfully accomplish them? An IMC Planning Grid™ helps to assess this in an integrated way.

It takes a lot of experience and judgment to build the illustrated chart. You have to be very clear in defining the objectives, and understanding where your customers or prospects are in their relationship with the brand.[9] If the job is to get more business from longstanding customers (through cross-sell and up-sell) this will lead to a very different grid than one designed to launch a new product to a new customer base.

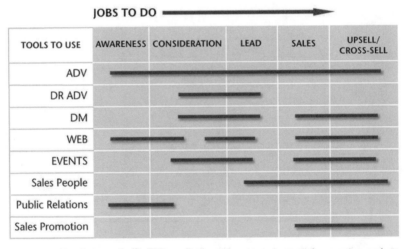

		JOBS TO DO ⟶			
TOOLS TO USE	**AWARENESS**	**CONSIDERATION**	**LEAD**	**SALES**	**UPSELL/ CROSS-SELL**
ADV	▬▬▬▬▬▬▬▬▬▬▬▬▬▬▬▬▬▬▬▬▬▬				
DR ADV		▬▬▬▬▬▬▬			
DM		▬▬▬▬▬▬▬		▬▬▬▬▬▬▬	
WEB	▬▬▬▬▬▬	▬▬▬▬▬		▬▬▬▬▬▬	
EVENTS		▬▬▬▬▬▬▬		▬▬▬▬▬▬	
Sales People			▬▬▬▬▬▬▬▬▬▬▬▬▬▬▬		
Public Relations	▬▬▬▬▬▬				
Sales Promotion				▬▬▬▬▬▬▬▬	

Upsell – Increasing the lifetime value by getting your customers to buy premium products (e.g. Green Amex Card to Gold).
Cross-sell – Increasing lifetime value by getting them to buy other products (e.g. selling Auto Flight Insurance to Amex Cardmembers).

---

9   Alan Middleton makes the same point, using the idea of where the brand fits in with the customer/prospect buying system.

Another useful tool is the Communications Architecture Triangle.™ It defines the role of each medium according to what it does best, with the idea that each "layer" increases the effectiveness of the layer below. For example, the lift in the response channels can be tested and quantified. If a direct mail package performs 50% better when supported by brand-driven TV advertising then the overall return is obviously improved.

Of course, the different media do not always fit so neatly into layers; they can have a role that spills into other layers. The point is to identify how each can help solve the communication task at hand, and to recognize that effort at a higher layer should increase the effectiveness of the activity below it.

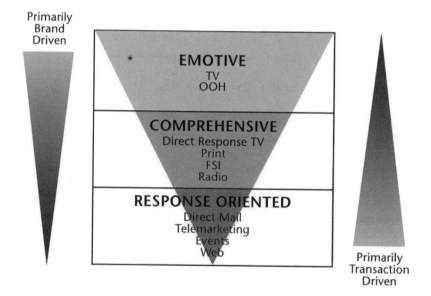

Either of these models, depending on the task, will help identify the channels, and the degree of effort that each should get. This helps eliminate discipline bias by linking decisions to objectives and outcomes. It also begins to answer brand messaging questions by assigning relative importance to each channel. It also encourages all players to think beyond media-driven solutions, and consider every point of contact.

d) *The Brand*

Every agency and most clients have their way of defining and describing a brand. It can be very difficult to disentangle all this. We've found that a better way is to use all that thinking to come up with what we call:

~ The Organizing Idea ~

It has to be broad enough that a single-minded television spot, a multi-paged brochure, or a decision about what to put on the side of delivery trucks can live comfortably with it. It reflects the brand as a collection of experiences, expectations and feelings, and in so doing the different disciplines don't argue over their inclusion or not. We have found that it is usually best expressed in words (not visuals) though of course it will eventually have to be captured by the appropriate look and feel for each channel.

In all this, it has to be a big idea. Not just the idea for an ad or a web application, but an idea that has the legs to take it everywhere it needs to go. IBM's communications are organized around the idea of solutions. It's not just hardware, software, and the services, it's how IBM combines it to work for you.

American Express is organized around the idea of the user's concept of success, and outstanding customer service. Motorola (a recent campaign that you may not yet have seen in Canada) used the Taiwanese shorthand for the phone—Moto. The word carried enough attitude for it to be an organizing idea.

e) Interpretation by Discipline

With the organizing idea in hand, each discipline can express the brand in a way that fits best with their channel. Take American Express. The user's concept of success demanded the high-end production values, rich visual imaging and celebrity spokespeople in such campaigns as "Do you know me?" in the 70s, and "Portraits" in the 80s. More recently, we've seen celebrities like Tiger Woods.

When this is translated to direct mail the celebrity spokespeople disappear. The audience expects to be treated like a member of a select group. Contact must be personalized, one on one, selectively issued. Not ads-reconfigured-for-the-mail.

A package using spokespeople would miss the point entirely, telegraphing an impersonal attitude from the brand, leaving our audience feeling unimportant, and not treated as individuals.

This is an area where it's easy to run into trouble. Some, wrongly in our opinion, integrate the advertising idea into other channels by replicating headlines and visuals. It's not about cutting and pasting images and copy. It's about including the signposts, the messaging and the feel of the brand in the way that best uses the discipline. It's *translating* the idea and the brand through different channels.[10]

f) Who Integrates?

It would be wonderful if everybody involved in IMC loved all disciplines as if each were their own child. Unfortunately, that's not the reality. In our experience you can cross-train account management, media and production. But creative folk? Forget it. Very few can do all disciplines well. The best bet is to keep creative people focused in their respective disciplines, working to the "organizing idea."

---

10 This metaphor of translation is excellent. If we just translate *words* from one language into another, we miss the mark entirely. We have to capture the *meaning*.

Angus Jenkinson at the Luton Business School in the UK said it best when he wrote:

> Integrated marketing should be fertile. Instead of repetition let us think of harmony and variations on a theme. Perhaps even instead of consistency, let us think of coherence or integrity.[11]

g) Keep Testing

The planning charts can only do their job if they are continually refreshed with new information and in-market learning. What's the optimal media recipe by channel? Has our customer's relationship with the brand evolved? Have competitive or environmental conditions changed? At the end of the day, in-market testing (with the right metrics in place) provides the best illumination on where to go next. Once again let's take a look at American Express.

---

11 The Centre for Integrated Marketing is on the leading edge of UK thinking. Angus Jenkinson is Professor of Integrated Marketing there.

Brand television advertising has always dramatically lifted the response rates of Take Ones, Free Standing Inserts and Direct Mail (by up to 100%).

Self-select channels (where consumers take the initiative, such as DRTV, FSIs and Take Ones) have always generated more profitable customers than pre-select channels such as direct mail. Conventional wisdom, reasonably enough, is that if you self-select you are more committed, and consequently more profitable as a customer. However, we've started to see pre-select channels outperform self-select channels. It seems that the proliferation of credit card applications has reduced the relevance or necessity for self-select channels. So the IMC mix is shifting away from Take Ones and FSIs, towards direct mail and other low cost channels—with better results over time.

h) Nurture the Brand over Time

Continuous testing is the pragmatic aspect of this, but there is an equally important attitudinal component. Do the key players on the team understand (deep in their bones) the brand, historically, now and into the future. The pressures for short-term fixes are immense, and often valid, but they can distract from this. Keeping this vision alive is a key role for the leader on the client and agency sides.

i) Marketing the Brand Inside the Client Organization

This is critical. Does the entire organization understand what the brand stands for, and what they have to do to make that come true at every point of contact? [12] Between 1990 and 1995, British Airways flew every employee from around the world, to London, in batches of 100, to explain the idea behind the World's Favourite Airline campaign. The brand idea wasn't just about serving business travellers. It meant treating coach passengers (World Traveller Class) with great respect and dignity, because their once a year trip most likely had more emotional impact than any trip a frequent business traveller took. And British Airways was the world's most profitable airline during that era.

---

12 A store-check to a retail outlet revealed a refreshingly honest response from a store manager. Asked what his role was in executing the head office vision of "the brand" he replied, "I keep my head down, and fill out the forms."

j) Partnership

Tearing down silos is vital, but so too is building genuine partnership between client and agency. Angus Jenkinson articulated it well:

> Trust and understanding (are) both powerful principles of integration; the politics of power and conflict are a hindrance.

In Conclusion

In trying to build great brands, we all have enormous complexity to consider, not least of which is the relentless pressure to outsmart competitors while delivering the bottom line. But customers are blissfully unconcerned by this. They expect great brands to understand and meet their needs, and behave in a way that earns their trust and respect. IMC, properly done, keeps this centremost in our minds.

Bibliography

Duncan, T., & Moriarty, S. (1997). *Driving Brand Value: Using Integrated Marketing to Manage Profitable Stakeholder Relationships*. New York: McGraw Hill.
Jenkinson, A. (2002). *Integrated Marketing – Radical Ideas for a New Vision*. Luton: Centre for Integrated Marketing, University of Luton.
Ogilvy & Mather Worldwide. (2002). *360 Degree of Brand Stewardship*.

Angus Jenkinson is a leading UK academic and consultant. You can access some of his work via www.luton.ac.uk

Tom Duncan is the founder of the IMC program at Colorado-Boulder. He worked for Leo Burnett before moving into academics and consulting. See www.colorado.edu/Journalism/sjmcgrad/imc/Site_Pages/fac.html.

Overview: Chapter Eleven

This chapter is about media convergence.

As most readers know, this idea created an immense bandwagon effect. It led to a flurry of corporate takeovers, and a great deal of re-thinking in the media community.

Now there has been time for the smoke to clear, and Hugh Dow puts it all in perspective.

He sees a definite role for convergence, but not as the be all and end all. For the right clients, though, using convergence in the right way, he paints a very positive picture.

Chapter Eleven

Media Convergence.
Lessons Learned. The New Reality.

HUGH DOW

Introduction

Seldom has a single word created such industry upheaval, such debate, such soul searching. Seldom has a single word affected the media business throughout the world to the extent the word convergence has. Entering our media vernacular in the late 90s the term convergence is still very much with us some four to five years later. Hardly a week goes by that the topic is not the subject of a newspaper article, or the content of some media luminary's speech.

Naturally, in five years a lot has changed. The early visionaries have had to face the reality of implementation. This has not been easy as many players will attest. Advertisers have explored the inherent opportunities of convergence. Many lessons have been learned by both media sellers and buyers. The realities of using convergence in the consumer communication mix are starting to emerge.

The Beginnings – The Visions

Initially, convergence was used as rationale for the spate of media acquisitions at the turn of the millennium. The AOL/Time Warner deal in the US was followed in short order in Canada by Global Canwest's purchase of Southam Newspapers and BCE's acquisition of CTV and the Globe & Mail. Quebecor used convergence to support the acquisition of the TVA television network and the Videotron cable business.

Those involved promoted a vision of the seamless integration of content with a variety of communication channels. This would provide consumers with greater choice in access to a wide menu of entertainment, information and communication. The fusion of content and distribution would generate superior operating and efficiency economies for the media owners.

From an advertising perspective, convergence was purported to provide one-stop shopping. An extensive basket of media goodies—television spots, newspaper pages, website banners etc. would be available from a single media owner. Supposedly, there would be a great demand from advertisers for such a concept. This would be accompanied by a whole new revenue stream for media owners.

Some Hindsight

Today, looking back, the whole theory of convergence was poorly conceived. Not perhaps in terms of the concept, but certainly in terms of its practical business implementation.

To believe that a collection of often diverse business silos could easily and effectively be cobbled together into one cohesive unit was, to say the least, misguided. Clearly, there was little understanding of the politics, the territories and the revenue-sharing issues involved. To believe that the advertiser would pay more for convergence, or that a new source of revenue would be generated, was simply unrealistic.

Perhaps the greatest challenge historically and even today has been in defining exactly what convergence is. There is no one standard industry definition—each player using and developing their own. This has presented enormous challenges particularly for the media owner's sales and marketing teams. To operate under a directive such as "We cannot really define it, but get out there and start selling it" has been difficult and confusing, both for sellers and buyers.

But All Is Not Lost

In spite of enormous challenges, the inevitable naysayers, the told you so's, and the departed visionaries, convergence is still alive and kicking. Sometimes it goes by another name—integrated sales, or multiplatform buys etc., but it is still convergence based and related.

Great progress has been made by the media owners in assembling convergence sales and marketing specialist teams. Sometimes recruited from the media buying side of the business, these teams have the mandate and authority to coordinate and provide offerings across a media owner's portfolio. The sales teams are developing multi-media experience (a new arena for many of the them) and are also appreciating the critical role of content in convergence programming. This is an enormously important component of convergence that will be covered in some depth later on in this chapter.

Examples or case histories of true convergence programs are few and far between. It is clear however that effective convergence programs will tend to be the domain of large advertisers, advertisers who have the resources to initiate and develop them, the funds to pay for them and, of course, the multi-platform creative to exploit the synergies. We were early explorers in the new land of convergence. With successful programs for advertisers such as RBC Financial Group, General Motors Cadillac, Microsoft and Johnson & Johnson/McNeil we are true believers in the concept. Properly conceived and executed, it can be an incredibly powerful communication tool. We'll share our learning in the rest of this chapter.

Convergence – A Definition

As a media management company, curious about the apparent opportunities in convergence, we struggled with what we were dealing with. After much internal debate and wordsmithing we developed a definition that we believe, from an advertiser's point of view, captures the essence of convergence:

> The content-driven integration of appropriate communication channels under the umbrella of a single or co-operating media owner(s).

Some background on this definition. First, "content-driven." As mentioned earlier, this is probably the single most important component of convergence. In fact, it is the primary driver. Content drives convergence and not the other way around. With a multi-media portfolio the media owner now has the ability to develop specific themed content across a variety of communication platforms. This enables the advertiser to position a commercial presence in environmentally suitable content. This is very different to the historic media owner silos where content consistency was next to impossible to achieve.

"Appropriate Communication Channels" is also an important distinction. Many prospective advertisers, it would appear, envisaged a scenario where they would be forced to purchase the entire contents of a media owner's portfolio. This clearly does not make sense and could well negate in the consumer's mind the advertiser's communication strategy. The correct course of action is to select only those channels that reach, and are relevant to, the target consumer. In our experience media owners realize this, and are flexible in terms of which of their properties are used in a convergence campaign.

"Single or co-operating media owner(s)" is a refinement we added fairly recently. Initially, our experiences were with a single media owner. Subsequent dealings revealed that no single media owner in Canada has a complete portfolio of media properties. Rogers is strong in magazines and radio, Canwest Global in television and newspaper, Bell Globemedia in television and on-line etc. etc.

With some trepidation we experimented with expanding a convergence campaign across two different media owners. We were pleasantly surprised to find this could work. With careful briefings and explanation of the content driver we discovered we could deliver a complementary mix of channels from the portfolios of two different media owners. We have now implemented two major convergence campaigns, each using two different sets of media owners. This significantly increases the complexity of developing a campaign, but it enables us to assemble the optimum combination of channels needed to surround the target audience.

Convergence – The Critical Criteria

In our experience convergence programs, to be truly effective, must deliver against four critical criteria. These are:

a) Content

This distinguishes convergence from a multi-media buy. It enables the advertiser to position a brand in a particularly appropriate environment. To be effective, this content environment must be unique and relevant to the target. To do this requires an in-depth understanding of this audience by both the seller and the buyer. The content must be consumer-driven—a far cry from the demographic-based media buy.

b) Synergy

The components of a convergence campaign must support and nurture each other. In practical terms this involves cross-promotion. Television is used, for example, to promote the upcoming special newspaper feature; newspapers drive prospects to the micro website etc. This requires an in-depth understanding of the target audience's relationship and usage of the communication channels involved. The goal is a scenario where the whole is greater than the sum of the parts.

c) Chronology

Timing in a convergence campaign, like many things in life, is everything. With what is invariably an extensive number of components, a decision must be made as to the sequence of exposure. Does the campaign kick off with the newspaper content? Do the television vignettes lead? When should the website be promoted? By crafting the components into a predetermined sequence the optimum timing, build and momentum can be achieved.

d) Channels

To effectively reach the target and to surround them with the chosen content requires a suitable mix of communication channels. Again, this requires an in-depth understanding of the targets, their media usage and their preferences. Sometimes a single media owner can provide the appropriate channel mix. Sometimes two media owners must be used to ensure a full spectrum.

Convergence Campaigns – A Model

In our experience there is a model that can deliver effective convergence campaigns. It is not a template, as each campaign must address the unique requirements at hand. It does, however, enable the development of a process that will deliver our definition of convergence.

Figure 1 depicts the essential components of the model. The centre or hub is the content component. Without this the model cannot work. It is the start point and unquestionably the most difficult to arrive at.

This content must be unique, in order to deliver maximum consumer impact. It must also be relevant to the audience, as it must be to the attributes and values of the brand or service involved. This requires in-depth understanding of the target audience together with the brand's marketing and advertising strategy. Finally, the content must lend itself to delivering across a variety of communication channels. In other words content that can be adapted to print, television, radio, the internet, etc.

Figure 1: The M2 Universal Convergence Model

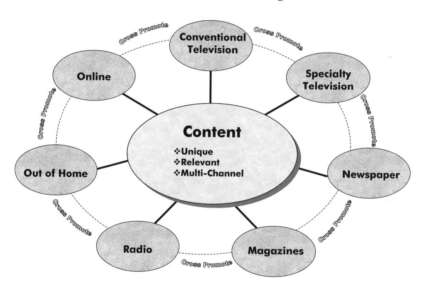

Content, Synergy, Chronology, Channels

There are no magic bullets for the easy development of this content. It requires both perseverance and perspiration. Generally, we have found brainstorming, and lots of it, produces the best results. Multi-discipline contributions from the advertiser, the agency and the media owner enable the gradual development of the content hub. It can, however, take months and not weeks before a satisfactory solution is arrived at.

Content is a new arena for advertising practitioners. Historically it has been the domain of the media owner, who has developed or purchased content with the hope of attracting advertisers and their revenue. With convergence, the advertiser is developing custom content together with the media owner. There is never any question as to fit, because it has been designed to do so right from the outset.

Once the content hub has been determined the communication channels can be evaluated. The goal is to surround the consumer with channels that they use and have positive relationships with. Not all of the channels in one media owner's portfolio might be suitable. Those that are not relevant should be excluded from consideration. With the candidate communication channels in place the content production teams can then begin their creative development work. How will the content theme be used in a television program? How can it work in newspaper editorial? How can it be incorporated into a website etc? The television producer, the newspaper columnist and the webmaster collaborate to arrive at content that reflects the central content theme.

The synergy or final closure that creates the rim of the wheel is the cross-promotion schedule. Because we are dealing with a single media owner this, in principle, is relatively straightforward. It is important because it weaves the various communication channels together and directs consumers to a website, an upcoming newspaper supplement, a television special etc. These cross promotions also provide carriage for a commercial exposure thus reinforcing the advertiser association or presence.

A wheel is a true example of synergy. The hub, spokes and rim are essential, but when assembled together the whole wheel is greater than the sum of the parts. In our experience this model works, and it has sufficient flexibility to encompass a variety of advertising and marketing scenarios.

The Cadillac Of Convergence Campaigns

The launch of General Motor's new Cadillac product line in Spring 2002 provided M2 Universal with an ideal opportunity to use a multi-platform convergence campaign to communicate a whole new positioning for the new Cadillac nameplates.

The primary objective was to develop a relevant, impactful program that showcased the 2002/2003 Cadillac line-up through association with leadership in technology, design and business.

a) It's All About Content

The media partner was Bell Globemedia. They were selected because of their extensive portfolio of communication properties, together with their interest in developing a true convergence campaign for a high-profile advertiser such as General Motors. Bell Globemedia assembled a team from their television, newspaper, magazine and internet holdings. Together with a team from M2 Universal and MacLaren McCann, we tackled the most critical driver for convergence campaign—the content. Often, we would have 25-30 people wrestling with how best to proceed with content development.

Content separates convergence campaigns from a conventional multi-media buy of spots and pages. After many weeks of research, debate, discussion and refinement we arrived at the Cadillac core content – Innovating Tomorrow. Subsequently we developed this into three specific pillars of Technology, Design and Business. This content theme matched precisely the communication platform for the new Cadillac product line.

Next came the challenge of developing television programs, newspaper and magazine editorial and website content for the three pillars of Innovating Tomorrow. The content was designed to address each of the pillars but developed optimally for each of BGM's communication channels. Cadillac commercial content, much of which was specially created, was then woven into the media content. It is important to note that BGM retained overall editorial control throughout the process.

b) Using The M2 Universal Model

Figure 2 illustrates how the M2 Universal model was applied to the General Motors Cadillac convergence campaign. The three pillars of the "Innovating Tomorrow" content theme were adapted for an extensive list of Bell Globemedia communication channels.

Figure 2: The General Motors Cadillac Convergence Model

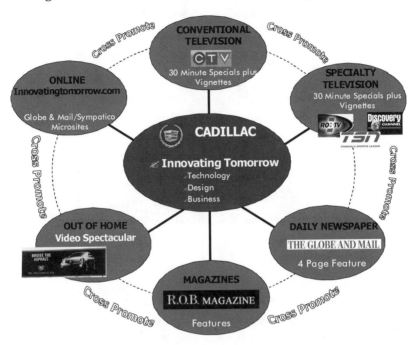

Content, Synergy, Chronology, Channels

c) The television content

Three thirty-minute journal format documentary television specials were created – one for each of the Technology, Design and Business themes. They were broadcast on the CTV Network, Discovery Channel and ROB TV. From each of the three specials, :90 and :120 second vignettes were created. The vignettes, which included Cadillac billboards together with brand sell commercials, ran extensively on the CTV Network, TSN, Discovery, CTV Newsnet and ROB TV. The vignettes were also used to promote and cross-promote the other communication channels. Some of the vignettes featured General Motors Executives and technical experts. A visual summary is on the next page.

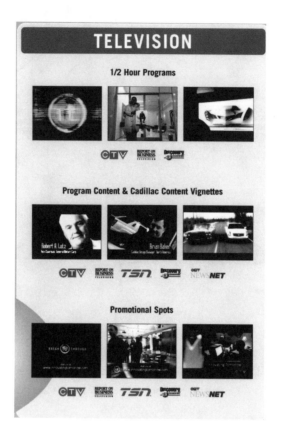

d) The Print Content

For print, three four-page newspaper supplements were developed – one for each of the three pillars. They ran in the Globe and Mail Report on Business section. Two of the four pages were full page Cadillac advertisements. Banner ads promoted the supplement and cross-promoted the television specials. The banner ads also directed readers to the website.

Bell Globemedia magazines were also used. Report On Business Magazine created editorial for each of the three pillars. The Globe Television Magazine alerted readers to the upcoming television specials. Full use was made of BGM's extensive media holdings.

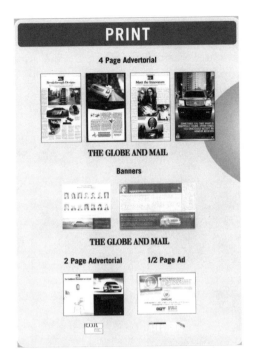

e) *Out-Of-Home*

A highly visible component of the campaign was BGM's Video Board spectacular at the intersection of Yonge and Bloor. This carried both promotional and commercial content.

f) Web Content

The Globe and Mail and Sympatico websites were an important component of the campaign. Not only did they provide consumers with content on the three pillars, but a microsite provided interaction, and an on-line contest. The grand prize was a brand new Cadillac CTS.

ONLINE

Microsite - Program & Cadillac Content, Vignettes

www.innovatingtomorrow.com

Contest   Promotional Banners

www.innovatingtomorrow.com

glebeandmail.com   Sympatico·ca

Connecting The Dots

The goal of convergence is that the whole is greater than the sum of the parts. With a multi-media owner this can be achieved through a careful crafting of cross-promotion opportunities. Not only do these lead consumers from one channel to another, they are an opportunity for advertisers to deliver message association. In the Cadillac campaign over 1,500 cross promotion connections were created. Each was chronologically crafted to build momentum for the campaign.

Lessons Learned

Convergence campaigns are not easy. They require commitment, tenacity and creativity from all concerned. Collaboration is the key, with constant communication between the client, the media owner and the agency. Without careful management, convergence campaigns can become a logistical nightmare. The area of content requires particular attention from the advertiser and agency, because it is so new to them.

Does Convergence Work?

We believe convergence programs, properly conceived and executed, can work. As we inevitably move into an era of increasing consumer control with technology for advertising avoidance we must move beyond our reliance on the conventional television commercial break. Convergence can deliver a content integrated presence that can be relevant to a specific consumer target group.

The Cadillac convergence campaign is still running at the time of writing, and the results have been impressive. Sales are strong and awareness tracking clearly shows the campaign is breaking through to consumers. Of particular note is the website traffic where the Cadillac purchase intender database is running at over 300% of the ingoing estimate.

Industry recognition of the Cadillac convergence campaign was recently received with a MIA (Media Innovation Awards) Gold in the Mixed Media over $1 million category. None of this success would have been possible without the encouragement and support of the General Motors marketing team and the unwavering commitment of the media team at M2 Universal.

Today "Convergence Bashing" would appear to be a popular media sport. Some media owners now deliberately avoid the use of the "C" word replacing it with terms such as "Integrated Selling." Others have walked entirely from the concept having disbanded their convergence units. Some media buyers conveniently sidestep the whole issue with a "prove to me that it works" response.

So why the industry disenchantment? And why are we so committed to the concept?

Convergence – The Realities

Initial industry expectations of convergence were way too high, fuelled largely by the media owner buying sprees of the late 90s. The pot of gold some owners envisaged, with media buyers lining up to buy baskets of spots and pages, never materialized. Secondly, too few players took the time to actually define the concept. As a result, few know what they were meant to sell, few knew what to buy. Those that persevered have found that convergence is politically difficult, incredibly time consuming, requires considerable creativity—but it is worth it when properly practiced.

So Why Does M2 Universal Believe?

- It enables us to better connect with target consumers through involvement with unique and relevant media content.
- It allows us to capitalize on the synergies available through cross-promotion of the communication channels involved.
- It provides the advertiser with a distinct and unassailable competitive edge.
- It enables us to depart from reliance on the conventional commercial break, which increasingly will be challenged by the new technologies such as PVRs.
- Finally and most important of all, convergence works. All measures we have seen, be they anecdotal or quantitative, point to dramatic results compared to conventional media placement.

But Are You Not Crossing The Line?

Convergence detractors invariably cite the "Church and State" argument. Advertisers should not be involved with content, consumers will see right through it, the integrity of the media is at stake, etc.

We believe that consumers appreciate smart, appealing content just as they appreciate the very best creativity in advertising. The key, of course, is developing content that is relevant, imaginative, and different. Then the advertiser involvement is recognized by consumers, is memorable and is positively regarded.

Some Important Implications

From our experience, convergence represents a sea change from the way we have historically conducted business. For example:

	Conventional	**Convergence**
Content	Media owners buy/create content hoping that it will be attractive to advertisers.	The buyer/advertiser works with the media owner to create content they know is relevant to audiences.
Structure	Content producers operate in isolation (i.e. silos) avoiding contact with their own sales groups and media buyers.	Content producers work with their sales team and the media buyer/advertiser. Content is relevant to the advertiser and the communication channel.
Creative	Creative development precedes the selection of appropriate communication channels.	Consumer knowledge and insights determine relevant communication channels for which creative can then be developed.

Convergence campaigns will tend to be the domain of a special group of advertisers. Product launches, repositionings and larger budgets have been the key drivers to date. There are, however, applications on a smaller scale and we intend to use our experience to work in exploring these.

Convergence is here to stay. It offers advertisers the opportunity to secure that all-important competitive edge. And it enables media owners to improve their share of advertising revenue, while developing a whole new relationship with the advertiser and the agency.

Index